THE SAGA OF IRELAND

TEST BOOK & ANSWER KEY

ISBN: 978-1-957206-25-7

Cover art by Chris Lewis of Baritus Catholic Illustration

CRUACHAN
HILL PRESS

Published by

Cruachan Hill Press
12552 E. Michigan Ave
Grass Lake, MI. 49240
www.cruachanhill.com

PRINTED IN THE UNITED STATES OF AMERICA

For Instructors: How to Use the Test Book & Answer Key

Structure

The Test Book and Answer Key contains one quiz for every chapter (the Introduction and Conclusion are not included). There are 35 quizzes in the book.

The quizzes are grouped into ten "units" thematically. Most units are comprised of four chapters; a few are three and Unit 10 is only two. Each unit has an essay question that deals with themes found throughout the unit.

At the end of the book is the answer key for quizzes and essays. The answer key for the essays is separate from the quiz answer key and appears after it.

Quizzes

Quizzes are either 15 to 20 questions in the following formats:

- Multiple choice
- Matching
- Fill in the blank
- Fill in the blank using a word box
- True and False

Whether the students take the quizzes "open book" or "open note" is up to your discretion.

If you want to add difficulty to the true and false, ask the student to explain *why* each answer is true or false.

Essays

Each unit has an essay question dealing with themes from that unit. It is recommended that students be allowed to complete essays open book and be given generous time to do so. It is recommended that essays be between six to nine sentences in length, but this is up to your discretion as well.

Sample essay answers are provided in the back. There is no uniform way to complete an essay correctly. The sample essay answers are meant merely to give an example of the scope and content that would be considered a satisfactory answer but are not meant to be replicated by the student exactly. Discretion is needed when assessing essays.

Unit 1: Introducing Ireland (Chapters 1-3)

Chapter 1: The Shores of Hibernia   / 15 = _____%

I. Multiple Choice: Select the best answer from the choices provided.

1. What was the Roman name for Ireland?
    a. Hibernia
    b. Emerald Isle
    c. Eire
    d. Iverni

2. What sea separates Ireland from Britain?
    a. British Sea
    b. English Channel
    c. Irish Sea
    d. North Lake

3. What is the most widely accepted theory of how Ireland became an island?
    a. Volcanic activity
    b. Plate tectonics
    c. Asteroid impact
    d. Sea levels rising

4. What does topography mean?
    a. The arrangement of the physical features of a land
    b. The practice of weather forecasting
    c. The analysis of population demographics
    d. The study of ancient civilizations

5. What is Ireland's largest river?
    a. River Lee
    b. River Shannon
    c. River Boyne
    d. River Liffey

6. What are lakes called in Ireland?
    a. Reservoirs
    b. Lochs
    c. Loughs
    d. Ponds

7. What is one of the things Ireland's first settlers made out of flinty rocks?
    a. Jewelry
    b. Weapons
    c. Pottery
    d. Ornaments

8. Where did most people settle in early Ireland?
    a. The northeast
    b. The central plains
    c. The southwest
    d. The western coast

9. What is one of Ireland's oldest archeological sites?
    a. Newgrange
    b. Stonehenge
    c. Mount Sandel
    d. Skellig Michael

10. How many counties are in Ireland?
    a. 5
    b. 109
    c. 13
    d. 32

II. True or False: Select whether each statement is correct or not.

11. _____ In Ireland, you say the word county after the county's name, as for example, "Galway County."

12. _____ Northern Ireland and the north of Ireland are the same thing.

13. _____ Ireland is roughly the size of the American state of Texas.

14. _____ Ireland is a lush, green country with many forests, animals, and plants.

15. _____ Ireland has a mild climate.

I. True or False: Select whether each statement is correct or not.

1. _____ Coiceda means thirds, representing the three ancient Irish regions.

2. _____ Meath is the only ancient region the Irish still recognize as a province today.

3. _____ Slighe Mor was a great highway that stretched almost the entire span of Ireland.

4. _____ In the 5th century, the most powerful Gaelic clan were the Uí Neill.

5. _____ Niall chose to save the weapons out of the burning building.

6. _____ The two branches of the Uí Neill were the Eastern Uí Neill and Western Uí Neill.

7. _____ Dairy cows were extremely important in ancient Ireland and were used as a measure of wealth.

8. _____ Cutting down hazel, oak, or holly trees was a privilege reserved to the nobility.

9. _____ Gaelic clothing was color-coded based on social rank.

10. _____ Social status was extremely important to the Gaels in ancient Ireland.

II. Match the term with the correct definition.

11. ___ Coiceda

12. ___ Tuatha

13. ___ Ogham stones

14. ___ Ringforts

15. ___ Rí tuaithe

16. ___ Ruirí

17. ___ Rí coiced

18. ___ Half-free people

19. ___ Freedmen

20. ___ Fianna

a. king of several kings
b. Provinces
c. People that are born free but are poor and dependent upon others
d. Freed slaves that handle their own matters but are still expected to work for a lord
e. Provincial king
f. Collection of households
g. King of the people
h. Warrior bands not attached to any king
i. Settlements enclosed within a circular wall of earth
j. Stones with important information carved onto them

I. Multiple Choice: Select the best answer from the choices provided.

1. How did the ancient Gaels pass down their religion?
   A. Through songs and poems
   B. Cave paintings
   C. Hieroglyphic inscriptions
   D. Fortune telling

2. The religion of the ancient Gaels can best be described as
   a. Monotheist
   b. Dualist
   c. Polytheist
   d. Atheist

3. What profession were considered especially close to the gods?
   a. Farmers
   b. Blacksmiths
   c. Fishermen
   d. Weavers

4. What number were the ancient Gaels fascinated with?
   a. 7
   b. 12
   c. 500
   d. 3

5. Which Druids were the most important?
   a. Bairds
   b. Filid
   c. Vates
   d. Fianna

6. Which Druids were seers who interpreted the will of gods?
   a. Bairds
   b. Filid
   c. Vates
   d. Oenach

7. Who were the lowest level Druids?
   a. Bairds
   b. Filid
   c. Vates
   d. Oblates

8. What did the Gaels call the beings that they believed were buried in the prehistoric mounds?
   a. Tuatha Dé Danann
   b. Sídhe
   c. Fir Bolg
   d. Fomorians

9. What was Tír nAill? (Also known as the Tír na nÓg or Mag Cíuin.)
   a. The sacred mound of Tara
   b. Ancient battlefield
   c. A Gaelic market
   d. A magical world

10. What body part did the Gaels like to collect from their enemies?
    a. Heads
    b. Eyes
    c. Feet
    d. Hearts

II. Fill in the blank with the correct word from the word box.

Sea	Cernunnos	Druids	Imbolc	Ériu
Bealtaine	Lughnasadh	Dagda	Dead	Samhain

11. A well-known father god was _____, which means "the good god."
12. One of the mother goddesses was _____, a goddess of abundance.
13. _____, the beast master, was one of the most well-known Celtic gods.
14. Donn was the god of the _____.
15. Manannán was the god of the _____.
16. _____ were priests, judges, philosophers, poets, sorcerers, and prophets.
17. _____ was the Gaelic new year, on November 1st.
18. _____ was the arrival of spring, on February 1st.
19. _____ was the festival of firc, on May 1st.
20. _____ was the beginning of the harvest season, on August 1st.

In a paragraph of six to nine sentences, explain how the concept of status was important in Gaelic society.

Unit 2: Christianization (Chapters 4-7)

Chapter 4: Arrival of Christianity   ____/15 = _____%

I. True or False: Select whether each statement is correct or not.

1. _____ Christianity existed in Ireland before St. Patrick arrived there.

2. _____ The Gaels and Gauls are the same.

3. _____ South Ireland was divided into Leinster and Connacht.

4. _____ The north of Ireland was dominated by the Uí Neill clan.

5. _____ All of the four most holy bishops met St. Patrick, except for St. Ailbe.

6. _____ Each of the quattuor sanctissimi episcopi spent time in Rome.

7. _____ Christianity likely came to Ireland from Gaul.

II. Multiple Choice: Select the best answer from the choices provided.

8. To whom did St. Patrick give a bell?
   a. St. Ciarán the Elder
   b. St. Ailbe
   c. St. Hilary of Poitiers
   d. St. Ibar of Beggerin

9. Who was sent by the Pope to be the first bishop of the Scoti?
   a. St. Patrick
   b. St. Columba
   c. St. Palladius
   d. St. Brigid

10. Who was not considered one of the "Four Most Holy Bishops"?
    a. St. Ailbe
    b. St. Déclán of Ardmore
    c. St. Ciarán the Elder
    d. St. Patrick

11. Who was left in the wilderness to die?
    a. St. Déclán of Ardmore
    b. St. Ailbe
    c. St. Ibar of Beggerin
    d. St. Ciarán the Elder

12. Who trained in the schools of the druids?
    a. St. Déclán of Ardmore
    b. St. Ibar of Beggerin
    c. St. Ailbe
    d. St. Ciarán the Elder

13. Who was ordained a bishop by the pope?
    a. St. Déclán of Ardmore
    b. St. Ibar of Beggerin
    c. St. Ailbe
    d. St. Ciarán the Elder

14. Who built a hermitage and lived alone in the wilderness.
    a. St. Déclán of Ardmore
    b. St. Ibar of Beggerin
    c. St. Ailbe
    d. St. Ciarán the Elder

15. What are the "Four Most Holy Bishops" sometimes referred to as?
    a. Ulster Saints
    b. Leinster Saints
    c. Connacht Saints
    d. Munster Saints

I. Multiple Choice: Select the best answer from the choices provided.

1. What is the name of St. Patrick's autobiography?
   a. Chronicles of Faith
   b. Letter to Coroticus
   c. Life of St. Patrick
   d. Confession

2. St. Patrick's father and grandfather were
   a. Lawyers
   b. Clergy
   c. Kings
   d. Merchants

3. How did Patrick know about the ship that he could escape on?
   a. He saw it from the mountain top
   b. Someone told him
   c. He saw it in a dream
   d. He read it in a parchment

4. Who was St. Patrick ordained by?
   a. St. Germanus
   b. St. Augustine
   c. St. Ailbe
   d. St. Ambrose

5. What did St. Patrick do on the Hill of Slane to anger the king?
   a. Light an Easter fire
   b. Built a stone fortress
   c. Planted foreign crops
   d. Conducted a military parade

6. What does Sabal Phadraig mean?
   a. The Abbey of Eire
   b. The Church of Patrick
   c. The River of Saints
   d. The Mountain of Wisdom

7. How did St. Patrick obtain the hill of Ard Mhacha?
    a. He defeated King Dáire in a battle of wits
    b. He traded valuable relics with King Dáire
    c. He tamed wild beasts that threatened Munster
    d. He healed King Dáire and his horses using holy water

8. What did Patrick rely on to serve as centers of evangelism?
    a. Castles
    b. Trading Posts
    c. Monasteries
    d. Ring forts

9. What did the Druids and Gaelic chieftains continually try and fail to do to Patrick?
    a. Kill him
    b. Bribe him with riches
    c. Convert him to their beliefs
    d. Exile him from Ireland

10. What tells us the story of a group of Patrick's converts who were attacked by brigands and enslaved after conversion to the Church?
    a. Patrick's *Epistle to the Druids*
    b. Patrick's *Letter to the Soldiers of Coroticus*
    c. The *Chronicles of Gaelic Raids*
    d. The *Tale of Mac Datho's Pig*

II. True or False: Select whether each statement is correct or not.

11. _____ Patrick was raised a Christian but did not take his faith seriously as a young man.

12. _____ Patrick bought a slave and made him tend sheep.

13. _____ Only two documents written by the hand of St. Patrick's hand have come down to us.

14. _____ King Lóegaire's Druids welcome Patrick, and they had a friendly alliance with him from the start.

15. _____ Armagh is the most famous church St. Patrick founded.

16. _____ Patrick was the first Christian missionary to focus on the north of Ireland.

17. _____ St. Ibar at first refused to recognize St. Patrick's authority.

18. _____ St. Patrick baptized untold thousands of Gaels and consecrated hundreds of bishops.

19. _____ Many of the bishops he ordained functioned as abbots simultaneously.

20. _____ The bishops of Britain were happy about St. Patrick's success and supported him in his mission.

I. Multiple Choice: Select the best answer from the choices provided.

1. St. Enda came from the royal house of
   a. Mide
   b. Airgíalla
   c. Munster
   d. Ulaid

2. St. Enda was converted under the influence of whom?
   a. St. Patrick
   b. St. Fanchea, his sister
   c. St. Briga, his mother
   d. St. Ibar

3. What did St. Enda *not* forbid in his monasteries?
   a. Fishing
   b. Lighting fires for warmth
   c. Using tools
   d. Sleeping on beds

4. What islands became home to flourishing monastic cities?
   a. Isle of Man
   b. Canary Islands
   c. Aran Islands
   d. Shetland Islands

5. Who did King Muiredach carry across three fields on his back?
   a. St. Brendan
   b. St. Brigid
   c. St. Patrick
   d. St. Finnian

6. St. Finnian founded which monastery?
   a. Clonmacnoise
   b. Kildare
   c. Iona
   d. Clonard

7. St. Finnian encouraged
    a. Public penances
    b. Standing cruciform
    c. Private confessions of sinful thoughts
    d. Collective penance services

8. Who did St. Brigid's father lease her out to?
    a. A Celtic warrior
    b. A pagan Druid
    c. A Viking chieftain
    d. A Catholic priest

9. What did St. Brigid do to irritate her father and make him sell her to King Dunlang?
    a. Give his goods to the poor
    b. Refused to marry the suitor of his choices
    c. Defied his authority and led a rebellion
    d. Ran away from her father

10. What did King Dunlang do to Brigid immediately after he bought her?
    a. Banished her from Leinster
    b. Demanded she renounce her faith
    c. Set her free to do God's work
    d. Forced her into manual labor

11. What did St. Ninnidh do after he gave St. Brigid her final communion?
    a. Embark on a pilgrimage to a distant land
    b. Renounce his religious vows
    c. Encase his hand in silver
    d. Retire to a life of religious solitude

II. Fill in the Blank: Fill in the blank with the correct word from the word box.

Penitential	Clonard	Conleth	Church of Oak	Limestone	Inishmore
	Half-free	Monasticism	Scotland		

12. It was _____ that revitalized Catholicism in Ireland.

13. St. Enda founded the monastery of Killeany on the island of _____.

14. The Aran islands were barely habitable, formed of solid _____, their bare cliffs lay exposed to the open ocean.

15. St. Finnian's church is called _____.

16. St. Finnian composed a _____, a book of penances to be given to penitents by their confessors.

17. As the daughter of a lord and a slave, St. Brigid was _____.

18. St. Brigid founded a church called Kildare, meaning "_____."

19. After his conversion, St. Enda crossed the sea to study under St. Ninnian in _____.

20. St. Brigid recruited a craftsman named _____ to be the first Bishop of Kildare.

Chapter 7: The Twilight of Paganism   / 15 = _____%

I. True or False: Select whether each statement is correct or not.

1. _____ St. Kevin stood cruciform so long a bird built a nest in his hands.

2. _____ Christian monks and pagan Druids didn't have anything in common.

3. _____ King Óengus was baptized by St. Columba.

4. _____ Diarmait mac Cerbaill is believed to be the first Christian High King of Ireland.

5. _____It is rumored that there were islands off the coast of Connacht that hadn't even heard of Christianity as late as the 12th century.

6. _____ The Convention of Drumceat resulted in the abolition of the bardic order in Ireland.

II. Multiple Choice: Select the best answer from the choices provided.

7. _____ Early Celtic Christianity was noted for its lack of
   a. Sacred texts
   b. Bishops
   c. Art
   d. Martyrs

8. This Irish king had his foot impaled by the staff of St. Patrick.
   a. King Cormac of Tara
   b. King Óengus of Munster
   c. King Fergus of Connacht
   d. King Eochaid of Leinster

9. What did St. Columba argue for at the Convention of Drumceat?
   a. Abolishing the bards
   b. Preserving the bards
   c. Expanding the powers of the Druids
   d. Banning all pagan traditions

10. How did King Domnall II get the power to disband the Druids?
    a. Imposed heavy taxes on the Druids
    b. Banished them from the kingdom
    c. Win the Battle of Moyrath
    d. Destroyed their sacred groves

11. St. Kevin's monastery was at
    a. Glendalough
    b. Clonmacnoise
    c. Killeany
    d. Bangor

12. Which region of Ireland remained pagan longer than the rest?
    a. Leinster
    b. Munster
    c. Connacht
    d. Ulster

13. What role did King Diarmait mac Cerbaill play in the early adoption of Christianity in
    Ireland?
    a. He resisted the Christian missionaries
    b. He was the first Christian High King of Ireland
    c. He led a rebellion against St. Patrick
    d. He was a prominent Druid opposing Christian conversion

14. What did King Óengus mac Nad Froích do when presented before St. Patrick?
    a. Resisted baptism
    b. Asked to be baptized immediately
    c. Consulted Druidic soothsayers
    d. Fled from the ceremony

15. What was the Bachall Isu?
    a. The episcopal crozier of St. Patrick
    b. A sacred text illustrated by St. Kevin
    c. The monastic complex of St. Columba
    d. The pagan ritual by which High Kings of Ireland were inaugurated

In a paragraph of six to nine sentences, explain the transition from Druidic paganism to Christianity in Ireland and the factors that led to Ireland's conversion.

Unit 3: The Golden Age (Chapters 8-11)

Chapter 8: Diarmait mac Cerbaill   ____/20 = _____%

I. Multiple Choice: Select the best answer from the choices provided.

1. This location was considered a sacred site for the crowning of kings
   a. Tara
   b. Clonmacnoise
   c. Kerry
   d. Temple na-Skellig

2. The Gaels believed that Tara was the royal seat of whom?
   a. Tuatha Dé Fomóir
   b. Tuatha Dé Sidhe
   c. Tuatha Dé Riada
   d. Tuatha Dé Danann

3. What did the ban-feis ceremony represent?
   a. A celebration of foreign alliances
   b. A demonstration of military prowess
   c. The strength of the Irish people joined to the fruitfulness of the land
   d. A display of magical powers by the druids

4. If an over-king became powerful enough, what could he install himself as?
   a. Ard rí
   b. Druidic High Priest
   c. Ollamh Erenn
   d. Chief Brehon

5. What did the Gaels do if there was not an Ard rí?
   a. Went without one until someone strong enough claimed the office
   b. Appointed a foreign ruler
   c. Established a council of elders
   d. Formed a temporary alliance with neighboring tribes

6. What new powers did a man obtain upon becoming Ard rí?
    a. Command over the Druidic Orders
    b. None; it was largely symbolic
    c. Access to hidden treasures of the land
    d. Control of the Military Tribes

7. Which statement is true?
    a. Diarmait was a Druid and opposed Christianity
    b. Ireland's first Christian High King was Conchobar mac Nessa
    c. The conversion of Diarmait led to a decline in Christian influence in Ireland
    d. Diarmait was born into a Christian family and is Ireland's first Christian High King

8. Which statement is **not** true?
    a. Diarmait was born of the Southern Uí Neill in Meath
    b. Diarmait helped establish the monastery of Clonmacnoise
    c. Diarmait died in peace at a good old age
    d. Diarmait's was the last king to participate in the ban-feis

9. Who told Diarmait, "Thou shalt be king tomorrow"?
    a. St. Ciaran
    b. St. Patrick
    c. St. Finian
    d. St. Columba

10. What did King Diarmait rule in the argument between St. Columba and St. Finian?
    a. The book's copy should be burned to end the dispute
    b. St. Columba owned the book and was in the right
    c. Both saints should share custody of the book and its copy
    d. St. Finian owned the book and was in the right

11. Who won the "Battle of the Book"?
    a. Nobody; both sides forfeited
    b. St. Finian and the Middle Uí Neill
    c. St. Columba and the Northern Uí Neill
    d. Diarmait and the Southern Uí Neill

12. Who succeeded King Diarmait as Ard rí?
    a. The High Druid of Ulster
    b. The King of Meath
    c. The King of Munster
    d. The King of Leinster

13. Who was the last King of Tara inaugurated under the old druidic rites of ban-feis?
    a. King Diarmait
    b. King Cormac mac Airt
    c. King Niall of the Nine Hostages
    d. King Brian Boru

II. Matching: Match the term with the correct definition.

14. _____Ard rí inauguration ceremony

15. _____Sacred hill in Meath

16. _____Gaelic kings inaugurated at Tara

17. _____Sacred standing stone

18. _____Church Diarmait and St. Ciaran built

19. _____Rulers of Meath

20. _____Influencers in Ulster and Connacht

a. Southern Uí Neill
b. Tara
c. Lia Fáil
d. Northern Uí Neill
e. Ban-feis
f. Clonmacnoise
g. Ard rí

I. Fill in the blank with the best answer.

1. After the bloody Battle of the Book, _____ repented by sailing overseas into exile.

2. Columba swore an oath before God to neither set foot or nor look upon _____ ever again.

3. The island in the Scottish Hebrides where St. Columba finally settled is called the island of _____.

4. Columba was so famous that he ordained _____ mac Gabráin the first known royal ordination anywhere in Britain or Ireland.

5. Columba made sure his monks were well-trained in the art of _____ of manuscripts.

6. St. Columba became known as the Apostle of _____.

7. He also persuaded the Ard rí to recognize the independence of Áedán's territories, effectively breaking the Scottish _____ off from Ireland.

8. In a way, St. Columba is not only the founder of the _____ in Scotland, but the founder of Scotland itself.

9. The Rule of _____ was the first known Irish rule to be written down.

10. Though the Lombards were Arians, Duke _____ liked Columbanus and offered him land to found a monastery.

II. True or False: Select whether each statement is correct or not.

11. _____King Áedán was the first Christian king in Britain and a strong supporter of Columba.

12. _____ Columba's rule tells us that monks of Iona divided their time between prayer, work, and study.

13. _____ King Brude was overjoyed when St. Columba visited and immediately let him into his fortress.

14. _____ St. Columba was first person in recorded history to see the Loch Ness Monster.

15. _____ Despite his oath, St. Columba did actually return to Ireland once, for the Convention of Drumceat.

16. _____ St. Columbanus was not very bright and struggled in school.

17. _____ St. Columbanus was encouraged to pursue a life of solitude and penance by an anchoress, so he went abroad and studied under disciples of St. Finnian of Clonard and St. Comgall for several years.

18. _____ At first, the Suevi were confused by Columbanus and his monks, but when they healed a sick woman with prayers, the Suevi began coming to the monks for healing and instruction.

19. _____ King Childebert II of the Franks would not let Columbanus settle in his domain.

20. _____The Frankish bishops and Queen Mother Brunhilda did not like St. Columbanus, so they had the king banish Columbanus and his Irish monks from Luxeuil.

I. Multiple Choice: Select the best answer from the choices provided.

    1. Who was St. Brendan?
        a. A monk
        b. A druid
        c. A bard
        d. A warrior

    2. What book tells of St. Brendan's life and voyages?
        a. The Chronicles of Brendan
        b. The Pilgrimage of St. Brendan
        c. The Navigatio Brendani
        d. The Lebhar Breac

    3. Who consulted the book of St. Brendan's voyages while making his own journey across the Atlantic?
        a. Leif Erikson
        b. Marco Polo
        c. Amerigo Vespucci
        d. Christopher Columbus

    4. This was one of Christian Ireland's earliest writers.
        a. St. Columba
        b. St. Dallán
        c. St. Brigid
        d. St. Ailbe

    5. What does the name Dallán mean?
        a. "Wisdom of the Hills"
        b. "Eternal Voyager"
        c. "Little Blind One"
        d. "Healing Light"

    6. Which is **not** one of St. Dallán's works?
        a. Amra Maewyn Succat
        b. Amhra Coluim Cille
        c. Amra Senáin
        d. Amra Conall Coel

7. What does illumination mean?
   a. Enriching a manuscript with artistic elements
   b. Clarifying a text's meaning with commentary
   c. Lighting up a room
   d. Conducting a religious ritual involving candles

8. What are two examples of Irish illumination in larger texts?
   a. The Aberdeen Bestiary and the Luttrell Psalter
   b. The Codex Amiatinus and the Utrecht Psalter
   c. The Lichfield Gospels and the Book of Armagh
   d. The Book of Kells and the Lindisfarne Gospels

9. What style were sacred texts decorated in?
   a. Hiberno-Romanesque
   b. Insular
   c. Anglo-Saxon
   d. Byzantine

10. These are stories of the heroes of Ulaid set during the reign of the legendary King Conchobar mac Nessa.
    a. The Mythological Cycle
    b. The Ulster Cycle
    c. The Historical Cycle
    d. The Fenian Cycle

11. These stories, believed to have come from Leinster, center on the family of the hero Fionn mac Cumhaill.
    a. The Mythological Cycle
    b. The Ulster Cycle
    c. The Historical Cycle
    d. The Fenian Cycle

12. These stories preserve ancient Gaelic genealogies, embellished with mythological elements to bolster the reputation of the king's dynasty.
    a. The Mythological Cycle
    b. The Ulster Cycle
    c. The Historical Cycle
    d. The Fenian Cycle

13. This cycle deals with the conflict between the Tuatha Dé Danann and the Fomorians.
    a. The Mythological Cycle
    b. The Ulster Cycle
    c. The Historical Cycle
    d. The Fenian Cycle

II. True or False: Select whether each statement is correct or not.

14. _____ A local church was ruled by an abbot or a bishop, but it was often administered by a coarb.

15. _____ St. Brendan and a band of monks went on a voyage across the Atlantic to find "the Land of the Saints."

16. _____ St. Brendan was ordained by a bishop who had been both a disciple of St. Patrick and a friend of St. Brigid.

17. _____ St. Brendan wrote Irish version of the hymn "Be Thou My Vision."

18. _____ St. Dallán was attacked and beheaded by the raiders—although, according to legend, God miraculously restored the head to his corpse after death.

19. _____ There were no true cities in Ireland until the coming of the Vikings.

20. _____ Ireland had no bishops; abbots entirely replaced bishops in episcopal government.

I. *Fill in the Blank: Fill in the blank with the correct word from the word box*

Northumbria	Columba	Canterbury	British Isles	Benedictine
Roman Empire	Oswald	Augustine	Anglo-Saxons	Britain

1. England and Ireland both belong to a cluster of islands called the _____.

2. England had once been part of the _____, unlike Ireland.

3. Roman settlers came to _____, mingling with the Celts to become the Romano-British.

4. The Germanic settlers of England became known as _____.

5. _____ had been sent by Pope Gregory the Great to evangelize the Anglo-Saxons.

6. King Ethelbert was impressed by Benedictine monks and gave Augustine land in _____ to build a church.

7. _____ was the northernmost of the Anglo-Saxon kingdoms.

8. Deeply impressed with the holy Irish monks, _____ abandoned his pagan upbringing, was baptized, and embraced the Catholic faith.

9. St. _____ appeared to Oswald in a vision the night before he was planning to battle Cadwallon for the throne of Northumbria.

10. In _____ monasteries, abbots exercised total control over their monks.

II. *True or False: Select whether each statement is correct or not.*

11. _____ The Saxons that were sent to help the British in battle saw how weak they were, turned on the British, and began plundering their lands.

12. _____ Unlike the Anglo-Saxons, the Britons were pagans.

13. _____ Canterbury would become the center of St. Augustine's mission and the head of all English churches.

14. _____ Augustine's mission was successful; many Saxons converted to Christianity, including King Ethelbert.

15. _____ St. Patrick of Canterbury is considered the father of English Christianity.

16. _____ King Oswald gave St. Aidan the island of Lindisfarne upon which to build his monastery.

17. _____ St. Oswald was killed by pagans and is considered a martyr.

18. _____ St. Aidan had the habit of retreating to Inner Farne and pray in solitude throughout Lent.

19. _____ The Irish kept a very regimented monastic rule; every hour of the day was accounted for, but the rules of the Benedictine monasteries were more open, allowing the monks greater discretion in how they spent their time.

20. _____ One of the few things that Benedictine and Irish monks agreed on was the date Easter occurred.

In a paragraph of six to nine sentences, explain how Ireland helped Christianity spread to nearby kingdoms and regions.

Unit 4: Foreign Conquest (Chap. 12-15)

Chapter 12: The Age of the Vikings   / 20 = _____%

I. True or False: Select whether each statement is correct or not.

1. _____ Pope Honorius sent the Irish a letter threatening them with excommunication if they did not adopt the Roman dating of Easter.

2. _____ The last Irish church to adopt the Roman calculation of Easter was that of Iona.

3. _____ The monasteries were independent of politics and did not have clan alliances.

4. _____ Irish monks were not averse to combat and sometimes took part in battles for the defense of their abbeys.

5. _____ Monasteries never got into battles with each other.

6. _____ Vikings generally left abbots alone because they feared their power.

7. _____ King Naille Caille led an army against Thorgest and defeated him in battle.

8. _____ Even during the Viking invasions, there were more battles among the Irish themselves than with the Vikings.

9. _____ Vikings only raided Ireland seasonally but had no interest in settling down there.

10. _____ Norse Vikings teamed up with the King of Ulaid and fought off a group of Danes trying to seize Dublin.

II. Multiple Choice: Select the best answer from the choices provided.

11. What disease swept over Ireland and killed thousands of people, especially in monasteries?
    a. Smallpox
    b. The Yellow Plague
    c. Cholera
    d. Typhoid fever

12. What kind of allegiances did most monasteries have?
    a. Noble allegiances
    b. Regional allegiances
    c. Religious allegiances
    d. Clan allegiances

13. Who were the seafaring people of Scandinavia who raided western Europe?
    a. Vikings
    b. Saxons
    c. Franks
    d. Normans

14. What did the Vikings do to the monastery of Lindisfarne?
    a. Established a trade partnership with the monks
    b. Renovated and expanded the monastery
    c. Attacked the monastery and destroyed the church
    d. Conducted peaceful negotiations with the monks

15. Why did the Vikings attack monasteries?
    a. They sought religious conversion
    b. They were not strongly defended and full of gold and silver utensils
    c. They were in search of valuable manuscripts
    d. They aimed to establish diplomatic relations

16. What were two of the first Viking forts?
    a. Eoforwic and Wintanceaster
    b. Dúachaill and Duibhlinn
    c. Kaupanger and Birka
    d. Jorvik and Hedeby

17. One of the most fearsome Viking warlords of the invasions was
    a. Thorgest
    b. Ragnarr Lothbrok
    c. Ivar
    d. Lagertha

18. What did the Viking tribes Dubgaill and Finngail battle over?
    a. Ownership of a magical artifact
    b. Access to trade routes
    c. Influence over neighboring kingdoms
    d. Control of the lands around Dublin

19. Who were the Culdees?
    a. Celtic warriors fighting for independence
    b. Viking invaders seeking new settlements
    c. Ascetics who looked back to the example of Ireland's early saints
    d. Druidic priests preserving ancient rituals

20. The Culdees' rule was called the
    a. Rule of Iona
    b. Rule of Armagh
    c. Rule of Lindisfarne
    d. Rule of Tallaght

I. *Select the best answer from the choices provided.*

1. About how many different kings were ruling Ireland during the 10th century?
   a. 100
   b. 125
   c. 150
   d. 175

2. What were the Irish requirements for succession to the throne?
   a. Come from a ruling dynasty
   b. Possess exceptional military skills
   c. Demonstrate mastery in poetry and politics
   d. Be considered holy

3. Who did King Mathgamain and Brian initiate a war with?
   a. The Vikings of Waterford
   b. The Normans of Dublin
   c. The Vikings of Limerick
   d. The Celts of Connacht

4. Who did Ivar make an alliance with?
   a. The Kingdom of Munster
   b. The Northern Uí Neill
   c. The Connacht Druids
   d. The Uí Fidgenti

5. Who was first on Brian's list of people to kill?
   a. The High King of Tara
   b. Ivar and his sons
   c. The Bishop of Armagh
   d. King Mathgamain

6. How did Brian become known as Brian Ború?
   a. He defeated a fierce boar named Ború in a hunting contest.
   b. He inherited the title from his father, Ború the Wise.
   c. He kept court at an old ringfort called Béal Ború.
   d. He discovered an ancient relic known as the Ború Stone.

7. While Brian Ború was king of the southern Ireland, who was king of the northern half of Ireland?

        a. Cormac mac Cuilennáin

        b. Niall Glúndub

        c. Donnchad mac Briain

        d. Malachy

8. How did Brian persuade the king in the north of Ireland king to resign his throne to Brian?

        a. Brian said it would keep Mide from descending into anarchy.

        b. Brian threatened him with war.

        c. Brian offered him immense wealth.

        d. Brian invoked a prophecy foretelling the northern king's downfall.

9. What did the peace of Brian Ború **not** bring about?

        a. the establishment of new libraries

        b. the creation of art

        c. the reemergence of pagan religions

        d. the flourishing of a new generation of poets

10. On what holiday day did the Battle of Clontarf take place?

        a. Maundy Thursday

        b. Good Friday

        c. Christmas Day

        d. Easter Sunday

II. Fill in the Blank: Fill in the blank with the correct word from the word box.

> Apostolic city   Dal Cais   Uí Dúnlainge   Eoghanachta   Norse
> Church   Province   Máel Muad   High King   Sulcoit

11. People in Brian's time were not local to Ireland but to their own _____.

12. The leaders of the _____ clan in the mid-10th century were two brothers, Mathgamain and Brian.

13. King Mathgamain and Brian Ború engaged the Vikings of Limerick at the Battle of

    _____.

14. Brian also fought and killed _____, the troublesome King of Munster.

15. Cashel was the ancestral fortress of the _____.

16. Brian was the first _____ of Ireland to rule anything close to a centralized, united kingdom.

17. Brian wanted to bring order to the Irish _____.

18. Brian recognized Armagh as the "_____" of Ireland, giving royal support to Armagh's claim to be the head of the Irish church.

19. The _____ had never submitted themselves to Brian and considered him an enemy.

20. The ruling dynasty of Leinster were the _____.

I. *True or False: Select whether each statement is correct or not.*

1. _____ Connacht was thought of as Ireland's national capital, despite Ireland not being united yet.

2. _____ Murtagh of Munster, Ruadhrí Ua Conchobhair of Connacht, Domnall Mac Lochlainn of the Northern Uí Néill, and Domnall Ua Maél Sechnail fought constantly.

3. _____ Ruadhrí Ua Conchobhair of Connacht killed Domnall Ua Maél Sechnaill.

4. _____ Murtagh proclaimed himself High King, despite the current High King's claim.

5. _____ King Murtagh donated the Rock of Cashel to the Church in order to prevent the Eoghanachta from reclaiming their power.

6. _____ Turlough broke Munster up into three smaller kingdoms—the Kingdom of Thomond, the Kingdom of Desmond, and the Kingdom of Osraige.

7. _____ Turlough Mór O'Connor ruined Ireland's central government and appointed kings to every town and province instead of one king ruling over everything.

8. _____ Turlough Mór O'Connor struggled against the Church and persecuted monks and bishops.

9. _____ St. Malachy became holy after converting from a life of sin.

10. _____ St. Malachy was the bishop of multiple dioceses simultaneously.

11. _____ Turlough O'Connor was the last Irish High King.

12. _____ The Cistercians Malachy brought back from St. Bernard founded the Abbey of Mellifont.

II. Matching: Match the term with the correct definition.

13. ____ Murtagh O'Brien

14. ____ Turlough O'Connor

15. ____ Cross of Cong

16. ____ Cong Abbey

17. ____ Gregorian Reform

18. ____ Synod of Cashel

19. ____ Synod of Ráth Breasail

20. ____ Athlone

a. Ornamented processional cross

b. Church gathering calling for reform

c. First stone castle in Ireland

d. Famous Irish church that still stands

e. Great-grandson of Brian Ború

f. Created Ireland's diocesan system

g. Movement to stop clerical immorality

h. Murtagh's nephew; Ruadhrí's son

I. Fill in the blank with the correct word from the word box.

Royal Constable	High King Rory	Leinster	Northern Uí Néill
Richard de Clare	Alexander III	Henry Diarmait	Waterford

1. Diarmait recruited _____, Earl of Pembroke to help him attack King Rory's army.

2. Strongbow attacked the prosperous town of _____ and stormed it, massacring 700 inhabitants.

3. _____ positioned his army outside of Dublin to intercept the invaders, but Diarmait and Strongbow went around him by passing through the Wicklow Mountains.

4. Rory killed Conchobar, the son of _____.

5. Strongbow claimed the throne of _____ after Diarmait's death.

6. _____sent Strongbow a message ordering him to return to England or all his lands would be seized.

7. Henry agreed to recognize Strongbow as _____ in Ireland if Strongbow handed over important towns and fortresses to the king.

8. High King Rory refused to submit to Henry, however, as did the rulers of Meath and the fiercely independent _____.

9. _____ recognized Henry as temporal lord of Ireland and encouraged the Irish to submit to him.

II. Multiple Choice: Select the best answer from the choices provided.

10. From whom did Diarmait ask for aid against Rory?
    a. King Henry II
    b. Queen Eleanor of Aquitaine
    c. Pope Alexander III
    d. Turlough Mor O'Connor

11. What did Henry do when Strongbow was ready to leave for Ireland?
    a. Offered him a royal title
    b. Provided military support
    c. Forbade him to leave England
    d. Granted him a fleet of ships

12. How did Diarmait lure King Rory into thinking he wanted peace?
    a. Launched a surprise attack during a peace negotiation
    b. Gave Rory hostages, including his own son
    c. Arranged a marriage alliance with Rory's family
    d. Offered Rory a very large payment

13. What did Diarmait promise Strongbow?
    a. · A chest of gold coins
    b. A fleet of warships
    c. A map to hidden treasures
    d. The hand of his daughter

14. What happened when Rory and Strongbow could not agree on a deal?
    a. They settled their differences through diplomacy
    b. Strongbow surrendered and returned to England
    c. A third-party mediator resolved the conflict
    d. Strongbow launched a surprise attack on Rory's army

15. Who was the High King in all Gaelic lands outside of Leinster, according to the Treaty of Windsor?
    a. Rory O'Connor
    b. BrianBorú
    c. Turlough O'Connor
    d. Murtagh O'Brien

In a paragraph of six to nine sentences, explain why the Irish were ultimately unable to unify their island into a single kingdom in the 9th-12th centuries. Make sure to use examples.

Unit 5: The High Middle Ages (Chap. 16-18)

Chapter 16: The Norman Age   / 15 = _____%

I. Select the best answer from the choices provided.

1. Who blatantly violated the terms of the Treaty of Windsor and pilfered Gaelic lands?
    a. Viking raiders
    b. Scottish clans
    c. Welsh warriors
    d. Norman lords

2. Which lands were not brought under Norman power?
    a. Ulster, Munster, and Connacht
    b. Leinster
    c. The Kingdom of Mide
    d. The Kingdoms of Osraige and Thomond

3. Who abdicated the high kingship in 1183?
    a. King Diarmait
    b. King Turlough
    c. King Rory
    d. King Donal

4. What title did King Henry want to give to his son, but Pope Lucius III refused?
    a. "Emperor of Britannia"
    b. "King of Ireland"
    c. "Duke of Normandy"
    d. "Prince of Scotland"

5. What caused Prince John's first trip to Ireland to have a rocky start?
    a. John fell ill upon arrival
    b. Bad weather disrupted the journey
    c. The Irish nobles rejected John's diplomatic proposals
    d. John insulted the Irish nobles' long beards

6. Why did King John return to Ireland?
    a. To conquer the Gaels
    b. To subdue the Anglo-Norman nobles
    c. To participate in religious pilgrimage
    d. To attend a royal wedding

7. King John promised King Cathal his friendship and security in exchange for what?
    a. For Cathal to provide military aid
    b. For Cathal to marry one of John's daughters
    c. For Cathal to swear fealty to John
    d. For Cathal to surrender his kingdom

8. The Normans made Ireland into an island of
    a. Towns
    b. Abbeys
    c. Cathedrals
    d. Trade

9. What was the Irish Parliament modeled after?
    a. The Viking Althing
    b. The Scottish Parliament
    c. The French Parlements
    d. The English Parliament

10. The Gael's religious system was centered around monasteries and abbeys, but what system did the Normans use?
    a. Druidic sacred groves
    b. Diocesan parish system
    c. A series of metropolitan eparchies
    d. Monastic communities

11. Who replaced the coarbs and laymen who controlled the Irish monasteries?
    a. Vikings
    b. Clergy
    c. Nobles
    d. Druids

II. Matching: Match the term with the correct definition.

12. _____ Treaty of Windsor

13. _____ Carlow

14. _____ Royal charters

15. _____ Cistercians

16. _____ The Magna Carta

17. _____ The Irish Parliament

18. _____ The Bruce campaigns

19. _____ Gaelicized

20. _____ The Pale

a. Norman walled town

b. Adopting Gaelic customs

c. An order brought to Ireland

d. Scottish attempt to conquer Ireland

e. Document allowing towns to trade

f. Irish land under English rule

g. Recognized Rory as High King

h. Created to maintain royal law

i. Guaranteed rights the king had to respect

I. True or False: Select whether each statement is correct or not.

1. _____ Three branches of the De Burghs fought each other for control of Ulster.

2. _____ Nobody won the Burke Civil War; they Burkes simply split into three smaller clans.

3. _____ The Bubonic Plague was brought to humans by bats in Asia.

4. _____ The plague killed 30-75% of those it infected.

5. _____ Sometimes entire villages would be wiped out down to the last person during the plague.

6. _____ The Church continued to function and hold Masses as usual throughout the plague.

7. _____ The chaos of the plague allowed the Irish reassume control over the lands formerly held by the English.

8. _____ During the Hundred Years' War, the Irish fought in France on the side of England.

9. _____ The Anglo-Irish were English in genealogy only; in every other respect they became indistinguishable from native born Irish.

10. _____ The Statutes of Kilkenny aimed to further mix the English and Irish, hoping both cultures would benefit from each other.

11. _____ The Statutes of Kilkenny were successfully enforced.

12. _____ The Earls of Kildare declined in importance during the 15th century.

13. _____ During the late Middle Ages, the Fitzgeralds married into the powerful O'Neill clan.

14. _____ Though the Fitzgeralds technically represented the King of England, in practice they were independent, doing as they wished.

II. Match the term with the correct definition.

15. ____ Edmond de Burgh

16. ____ Burke Civil War

17. ____ The Black Death

18. ____ The Hundred Years' War

19. ____ Statutes of Kilkenny

20. ____ Earls of Kildare

a. War fought between England and France

b. Disease that came from Asia

c. Rules meant to strengthen English identity

d. Drowned in Lough Mask

e. Powerful descendants of John Fitzgerald

f. The war between the De Burghs

I. Fill in the blank with the correct word from the word box.

Church of Ireland	Silken Thomas	Clanricarde	Young Gerald	England
Henry VIII	Wars of the Roses	Ireland	Poynings	Act of Supremacy

1. The Kingdom of England was in a civil war between the rival houses of Lancaster and York, each vying for control of the throne. This conflict was known as the _____.

2. Gerald Fitzgerald, Earl of Kildare, went to war against the _____, a fully Gaelicized branch of the Burkes who ruled southern Connacht.

3. When _____ found out about Fitzgerald's plot to murder them, he summoned a parliament and Gerald Fitzgerald was condemned for treason.

4. Gerald was succeeded by his son, known as "_____."

5. The very year Young Gerald resigned, King Henry VIII had passed the _____, wresting control of the English church from the pope.

6. _____ Fitzgerald boldly threw down his sword in an act of defiance against Henry VIII.

7. The Butlers made an alliance with _____ and promised to reduce the power of the Fitzgeralds and their allies.

8. All who would not swear allegiance to Silken Thomas Fitzgerald's rebellion were imprisoned, and he announced his intention to exile or slay every man within the Pale born in _____.

9. The _____ was established as an Irish duplicate of the Anglican church.

10. Henry VIII had succeeded in reestablishing English control in _____ after centuries of decline.

II. Select the best answer from the choices provided.

11. What did Henry Tudor marrying a Yorkist princess do?
    a. United the houses of Lancaster and Tudor under a new monarchy
    b. Led to the dissolution of the English monarchy
    c. Sparked a civil war between England and France
    d. Joined the houses of York and Lancaster in a new dynasty

12. Where was the only place where English custom and language were used in Ireland?
    a. Connacht
    b. The Pale
    c. The Midlands
    d. Munster

13. Who held the office of Lord Deputy?
    a. The Ormondes
    b. The Earls of Kildare
    c. The Butlers
    d. Clanricarde

14. Why didn't the Tudors trust the Fitzgeralds?
    a. Their support for the Tudor dynasty.
    b. Their independence and support of the Yorkists.
    c. Their alliance with the French.
    d. Their refusal to acknowledge the English crown.

15. What happened after Gerald Fitzgerald was removed?
    a. The Statutes of Kilkenny were reaffirmed
    b. The Fitzgeralds were excommunicated
    c. A new Irish Parliament was created
    d. Henry introduced English law to Ireland

16. According to an old Irish tale, the Great Earl Gerald Fitzgerald could do what?
    a. He possessed the ability to control the weather
    b. He had the power to heal the sick
    c. He could communicate with animals
    d. He could shapeshift

17. Who was Young Gerald in a constant feud with?
    a. Lord Kildare
    b. Lord Desmond
    c. Lord Ormonde
    d. Lord Thomond

18. What happened immediately after Silken Thomas Fitzgerald publicly renounced his allegiance to Henry VIII?
    a. He formed an alliance with other Irish lords.
    b. He beheaded the English emissary
    c. A harpist encouraged him by singing about his ancestors
    d. He sought refuge in France.

19. When Young Gerald found out about Silken Thomas's rebellion, what happened?
    a. He died of shock
    b. He joined the rebellion against the Tudors
    c. He entered a monastery
    d. He fled to Spain

20. Whom did Silken Thomas accidentally have murdered?
    a. John Alen, Archbishop of Dublin
    b. Sir Edward Poynings
    c. George Cromer, Archbishop of Armagh
    d. Lord Leonard Grey

In a paragraph of six to nine sentences, explain both (a) what were the Wars of the Roses, and (b) how did the rise of the Tudors impact Ireland during the 16th century?

Unit 6: The Reformation Era (Chap. 19-22)

Chapter 19: The Desmond Rebellion & Nine Years' War   / 20 = _____ %

I. Multiple Choice: Select the best answer from the choices provided.

1. What did the Crown of Ireland Act do?
   a. Established the Republic of Ireland
   b. Dissolved the Irish monarchy
   c. Created the title "King of Ireland"
   d. Granted Ireland full independence

2. What is a papal fief?
   a. A piece of land no-one can rule without consent of the pope
   b. A piece of land granted by a local lord
   c. A title given by the English monarch
   d. An area designated for religious worship

3. Who did Pope Paul IV recognize as co-monarchs of Ireland, therefore legitimizing the Kingdom of Ireland?
   a. King Henry VIII
   b. Queen Elizabeth I
   c. King Philip and Queen Mary
   d. Queen Mary I

4. Which of these was one the first English plantations?
   a. Sir Walter Raleigh's Estate in Cork
   b. Lord's County in Kerry
   c. Munster Plantation
   d. Queen's County in Laois

5. Who kept Shane O'Neill, son of the first Earl of Tyrone, from succeeding the throne?
   a. King James I
   b. Queen Elizabeth I
   c. King Charles I
   d. King Charles II

6. What were "lord presidencies"?
    a. Ecclesiastical territories governed by bishops
    b. Financial districts controlled by wealthy lords
    c. Administrative regions governed by earls
    d. Military governors appointed to keep peace among clans

7. Which two clans went to war against each other, despite Queen Elizabeth's insistence that the clans cease their in-fighting?
    a. O'Donnells and MacCarthys
    b. MacNeills and MacDowells
    c. Butlers and Fitzgeralds
    d. O'Briens and MacMahons

8. Who declared Queen Elizabeth a heretic?
    a. Pope St. Pius V
    b. St. Oliver Plunkett
    c. Pope Sixtus V
    d. Archbishop Thomas Cranmer

9. What is a Gallowglass?
    a. A native Irish poet
    b. A foreign mercenary from Scotland
    c. A medieval Irish dance
    d. A member of the English nobility

10. Who gave Earl Hugh weapons, money, and military advisors out of spite against England?
    a. King Francis I of France
    b. Holy Roman Emperor Charles V
    c. Queen Mary Stuart of Scotland
    d. King Philip of Spain

II. True or False: Select whether each statement is correct or not.

11. _____ Queen Mary was very interested in promoting Irish independence.

12. _____ One way the English attempted to exert power was by meddling in the dynastic squabbles of the Irish clans.

13. _____ Shane dealt Radcliffe an embarrassing defeat at the Battle of Red Sagums.

14. _____ James Fitzmaurice convinced the clans of Munster to join him in rebellion against England.

15. _____ Fitzmaurice led two uprisings against England and was successful both times.

16. _____ Fitzmaurice's last wish was to preserve his body until he could have a proper Catholic burial.

17. _____ The word Taoiseach means "chief" or "leader."

18. _____ Fitzwilliam had carried out the execution of 2,000 of the survivors of the Spanish Armada.

19. _____ The Burkes defeated the English, killing thousands of them.

20. _____ Despite his triumphs, Earl Hugh never managed to get inaugurated as The O'Neill.

I. Multiple Choice: Select the best answer from the choices provided.

1. What treaty restored peace in Ireland?
   a. Treaty of Mellifont
   b. Treaty of Kells
   c. Treaty of Cashel
   d. Treaty of Limerick

2. How did Catesby plan to kill King James?
   a. Kidnapping the king
   b. Poisoning the king's food
   c. Assassination during a royal procession
   d. Blowing up Parliament

3. What day commemorates the failure of Catesby's plot to kill King James?
   a. The Gunpowder Plot Day
   b. The Treason Day
   c. Guy Fawkes Day
   d. The Parliament Day

4. Who led the Flight of the Earls?
   a. The Fitzgeralds
   b. The Butlers
   c. Hugh O'Neill and Rory O'Donnell
   d. Edmund and Thomas Burke

5. What does the Flight of the Earls represent?
   a. A successful rebellion against English rule
   b. The end of the Gaelic nobility in Ireland
   c. The establishment of a Gaelic kingdom
   d. A period of peace and stability

6. When were the English authorities ordered to apologize to O'Doherty for his treatment?
   a. As O'Doherty began his rebellion
   b. After O'Doherty's death
   c. Before O'Doherty's rebellion
   d. During negotiations for the Flight of the Earls

7. At the time of the Flight of the Earls, what was the majority religion in Ulster?
    a. Protestantism
    b. Druidic paganism
    c. Presbyterianism
    d. Catholicism

8. What is a Bill of Attainder?
    a. A bill establishing a new tax
    b. A bill granting titles of nobility
    c. A bill pardoning criminals
    d. A bill declaring someone an enemy of the state

9. What did Chichester require of all settlers on the Ulster plantations?
    a. They be fluent in Gaelic
    b. They be English speaking and Protestant
    c. They be proficient in archery
    d. Be willing to adopt Gaelic customs

10. Who were almost never given land in the Ulster plantations?
    a. English settlers
    b. Protestant settlers
    c. Scottish settlers
    d. Irish settlers

II. True or False: Select whether each statement is correct or not.

11. _____ King James I was a devout Catholic and did everything he could to grow his faith in Ireland.

12. _____ The Gunpowder Plot made the situation for English and Irish Catholics even worse.

13. _____ When Cahir O'Doherty protested his poor treatment, he was slapped in the face by the English governor.

14. _____ Hugh and Rory spent the rest of their lives planning to return to Ireland, but never did.

15. _____ Ulster was the smallest of the English plantations.

I. Fill in the blank with the correct word from the word box.

Ormonde   Kilkenny   Protestant   Conspirators   Royalist   Parliamentarians
Bann   Drogheda   Irish Catholics   Confederates   Strafford   Cromwell

1. To Puritans, _____ were barbarians, savages from a wild and uncivilized country.

2. The Parliamentarians passed a bill of attainder condemning the Earl of _____ to death.

3. Irish Catholics decided to seize power in Ireland, drive out the English, and eradicate the _____ plantations.

4. A group of Catholic _____ went to a pub in Dublin, got drunk, and loudly discussed their plans, ruining everything.

5. In Portadown, the Irish rounded up one hundred English settlers and threw them off a bridge into the River _____.

6. With Cromwell's help, the _____ defeated the Royalists in 1648.

7. The _____ and Ormonde signed a truce so they could oppose Cromwell together.

8. _____ and the Confederacy controlled all Ireland except for Dublin, Cork, and the surrounding regions.

9. One of Cromwell's objectives was to defeat the last outposts of _____ resistance in Ireland.

10. Cromwell killed about 3,000 people in the massacre of _____.

11. _____ returned to England in 1650 to begin a war against the Scots.

12. After the loss of _____, the Protestant Royalists serving under the Earl of Ormonde realized they could not win.

II. Matching: Match the term with the correct definition.

13. ___ Book of Common Prayer

14. ___ Covenant

15. ___ Royalists

16. ___ Confederates

17. ___ Laggan Army

18. ___ Owen Roe O'Neill

19. ___ Presbyterians

20. ___ Rinuccini

a. Only one capable of beating Cromwell

b. Charles tried to force it upon the Scots

c. Irish Catholic rebels

d. Calvinists against the Anglican Church

e. Militia of Ulster Protestants

f. Forces loyal to King Charles

g. Papal nuncio to the Confederacy

h. Pledge against Charles' Scotch reforms

II. Fill in the blank with the correct word from the word box.

Charles II	William III	Oliver Plunkett	Test Act	King of England
Jacobite	Enniskilliners	Penal	Charles Coote	Williamites

1. After Cromwell's death, the English Parliament was restored and _____ became king.

2. The leader of Royalist forces in Ireland who helped restore the Stuarts was none other than _____, the former Cromwellian commander.

3. The government passed the _____, requiring all persons serving in public office to receive Holy Communion in the Church of England and deny transubstantiation.

4. _____ was condemned and executed for treason "for promoting the Roman faith."

5. William of Orange was proclaimed _____ by Parliament.

6. The movement to support James was called the _____ movement.

7. Called "_____," Protestants organized themselves into military units and fought for William or Orange.

8. The _____were Ulster Protestants who formed cavalry units.

9. The word _____ means "punishment" or "penalty."

10. After James III was dethroned, Catholics were required to take an oath of allegiance to the new Protestant monarch, King _____ of England.

II. True or False: Select whether each statement is correct or not.

11. _____ One out of every five people in Ireland died as a result of the wars of the 17th century.

12. _____ Upon his return from Ireland, the Puritans dissolved the English Parliament and appointed Cromwell Lord Protector for life.

13. _____ Charles II offered to give Irish Catholics all of their land back and grant them seats in Parliament.

14. _____ The Treaty of Limerick disbanded the Williamite armies.

15. _____ The Penal Laws were meant to inflict a series of penalties upon Catholics to keep them impoverished and without political voice.

16. _____ The papacy announced its opposition to the Jacobite cause, telling Catholics to pledge allegiance to William.

17. _____ Priest shortages were common; some villages went months or years without a regular Mass.

18. _____ Converting from Catholicism to Protestantism was forbidden on pain of losing all property, legal rights, and imprisonment at the pleasure of the monarch.

19. _____ Catholics were forbidden from sending their children abroad for education.

20. _____ Catholics were not allowed to own a horse valued over £5.

In a paragraph of six to nine sentences, explain how the Cromwellian conquest of Ireland and the imposition of the Penal Laws shaped the social and political landscape of Ireland, and what were the lasting consequences on the Irish population?

Unit 7: The Age of Reform (Chap. 23-26)

Chapter 23: The Anglo-Irish   / 20 = _____ %

I. Multiple Choice: Select the best answer from the choices provided.

1. Who first carved out the Pale as a center of English power?
   a. The Vikings
   b. The Gaels
   c. The Normans
   d. The Anglo-Saxons

2. What is often said about the Anglo-Normans?
   a. They were more Irish than the Irish themselves
   b. They were more Scottish than the Scots themselves
   c. They were more Welsh than the Welsh themselves
   d. They were more Norse than the Norse themselves

3. Who did the strongest resistance to English rule come from?
   a. Native Irish clans
   b. English settlers
   c. Anglo-Irish families
   d. Viking warlords

4. How were those who fought against England treated?
   a. They were knighted
   b. They were granted additional lands
   c. Their lands were confiscated
   d. They were given titles of nobility

5. What were Protestant Anglo-Irish allowed to do?
   a. Vote in elections
   b. Own land
   c. Sit in Parliament
   d. All of the above

6. Why did Jonathon Swift start writing?
    a. He was bored with his work
    b. He was inspired by the works of Shakespeare
    c. He sought to improve his financial status
    d. He aimed to impress Queen Anne

7. What kept Swift from securing a better assignment in England?
    a. King George I's disapproval
    b. Queen Anne's dislike for him
    c. The influence of the Irish Parliament
    d. His refusal to conform to societal norms

8. What did Jonathan Swift's writings earn him?
    a. Banishment from Ireland
    b. A position in the English Cabinet
    c. A reputation as an Irish patriot
    d. An invitation to the Royal Court

9. What was rumored about Edmund Burke?
    a. He was secretly a Protestant
    b. He was secretly an atheist
    c. He was secretly a Jacobite
    d. He was secretly a Catholic

10. Who earned a reputation as a pro-Catholic politician, resulting in him becoming disliked?
    a. Richard Brinsley Sheridan
    b. Edmund Burke
    c. Charles James Fox
    d. William Pitt the Younger

11. Who admired Burke's writings so much that he had them all translated into French?
    a. King Louis XVI
    b. Napoleon Bonaparte
    c. Voltaire
    d. Catherine the Great

12. How did Henry Grattan begin his career in politics?
    a. By advocating for the reestablishment of Gaelic as the official language
    b. By promoting increased English influence in Irish affairs
    c. By opposing the existence of the Irish Parliament
    d. Pressing for independence for the Irish Parliament

13. The Catholic Relief Act of 1791
    a. Allowed Catholics to sit in Parliament
    b. Restored Catholic lands that had been stolen
    c. Restored Catholics' freedom of worship in England and Ireland
    d. Restored the Catholic hierarchy with Parliament choosing bishops

14. Swift's *A Modest Proposal* was meant to
    a. Draw attention to the poor treatment of Irish Catholics
    b. Show why Catholics should be allowed at university
    c. Argue that Catholicism should be restored as the official religion
    d. Literally argue for eating babies

II. Matching: Match the term with the correct definition.

15. ___ The Acts of Union

16. ___ *A Modest Proposal*

17. ___ The Catholic Relief Act

18. ___ Edmund Burke

19. ___ Irish Volunteers

20. ___ The Repeal Act of 1782

a. Militia to defend Ireland against France

b. Famous Anglo-Irish author

c. Written by Jonathan Swift

d. Joined England and Scotland

e. Restored freedom of worship to Catholics

f. Made Irish Parliament independent

I. Multiple Choice: Select the best answer from the choices provided.

1. Which monarch did the French Revolutionaries overthrow in 1789?
    a. Louis XV
    b. Louis XVI
    c. Charles X
    d. Napoleon Bonaparte

2. Why would many landlords throw small farmers off their land?
    a. To turn the land over to cattle grazing
    b. To establish a system of tenant cooperatives
    c. To encourage diversified agriculture
    d. To promote industrial development

3. What United Irishmen leader single-handedly convinced France to support a rebellion in Ireland?
    a. Wolfe Tone
    b. Thomas Russell
    c. Lord Edward Fitzgerald
    d. Napper Tandy

4. This victor at Ballinamuck also played an important role in American history.
    a. Thomas Gage
    b. Thomas Paine
    c. Charles Cornwallis
    d. Robert Dinwiddie

5. Which of these things did the Act of Union **not** do?
    a. Abolish the Parliament of Ireland
    b. Merge the Churches of England and Ireland
    c. Promise to work towards Catholic emancipation in Ireland
    d. Put an end to the Rising of 1798

6. Who fiercely denounced the Act of Union, believing it would weaken Irish culture?
    a. John Philpot Curran
    b. Henry Grattan
    c. Henry Flood
    d. William Ponsonby

7. Who was one of the most influential figures in the 19th century movement for
   Catholic emancipation?
   a. Rober Emmet
   b. Lord Castlereagh
   c. Daniel O'Connell
   d. Wolfe Tone

8. What did Daniel O'Connor believe about Catholicism and Ireland?
   a. He believed Catholicism had no relevance to Irish identity
   b. He believed Protestantism was the true faith of Ireland
   c. He believed Catholicism was central to Irish identity
   d. He believed Irish identity should be completely secular

9. Why did Daniel O'Connell declare that Irish Catholics should be content to
   "remain forever without emancipation"?
   a. He believed Irish Catholics were already treated equally
   b. He didn't want British government interfering with Irish bishops
   c. He believed Irish Catholics should strive for more political power
   d. He thought the Irish Parliament would grant emancipation without
      agitation

10. What kept Daniel O'Connell from taking his seat in County Clare?
    a. His refusal to renounce Anglicanism
    b. His lack of popular support
    c. His imprisonment for sedition
    d. The Oath of Supremacy excluded Catholics

II. Matching: Match the term with the correct definition.

11. ___ John D'Esterre	a. Daniel O'Connell
12. ___ The Peep O'Day Boys	b. Protestants who wouldn't go to the state church
13. ___ Orange Order	c. Created the United Kingdom
14. ___ Non-Conformists	d. Secret society opposed to Penal Laws
15. ___ Society of United Irishmen	e. Repealed Oath of Supremacy
16. ___ The Act of Union	f. Nationalists who opposed O'Connell
17. ___ The Catholic Association	g. Pledged to defend Protestant power
18. ___ Roman Catholic Relief Act	h. Killed by Daniel O'Connell in a duel
19. ___ The Liberator	i. Founded by O'Connell
20. ___ Young Ireland	j. Made night raids against Catholics

I. Fill in the blank

1. To make the Irish equal with voters in _____, the law raised the property requirements in Ireland to £10, a 500% increase.

2. Tenant farmers were _____, meaning they had no political path to address their concerns.

3. The _____ was caused by farmers' frustration with the government over the taxes they paid to support the Church of Ireland.

4. Though Irish Catholics now enjoyed freedom of religion, the Protestant Church of _____ remained the official church of the country.

5. _____ were introduced to Ireland during the Tudor era, likely by the Spaniards.

6. The British government tried to help the famine by lightening _____ on imports of grain.

7. Prime Minister John Russell was a member of the _____ Party, which meant he believed the economy would regulate itself without government interference.

8. The Irish _____ of 1847 stated that no Irishman could receive aid if he owned more than ¼ an acre of land.

II. True or False: Select whether each statement is correct or not.

9. _____ New industrial machinery that turned wool into clothing made it more lucrative to graze sheep than to use land for farming.

10. _____ The Catholic Church of Ireland imposed a tithe, or a tax, to support the church that everyone had to pay, regardless of religion.

11. _____ *An Gorta Mór* means "The Great Hunger"

12. _____ The penalty for not paying the Church of Ireland tithe was death.

13. _____ Potatoes were a staple of the Irish diet.

14. _____ Patt Lalor's plan to fight back against the Tithe Law failed.

15. _____ During the potato famine, millions Irish simply left the country, migrating to the United States, Canada, or Australia.

I. Multiple Choice: Select the best answer from the choices provided.

1. What did the Fenian Brotherhood hope to do?
   a. Establish a monarchy in Ireland
   b. Advocate for continued British rule
   c. Start a rebellion in Ireland.
   d. Promote cultural assimilation.

2. Who formed the Irish Republican Brotherhood (IRB)?
   a. James Stephens
   b. Michael Davitt
   c. Charles Stewart Parnell
   d. John Devoy

3. Which two organizations formed an alliance?
   a. The IRB and the Young Ireland movement
   b. The Fenian Brotherhood and the Orange Order
   c. The Land League and the Home Rule League
   d. The IRB and the Fenian Brotherhood

4. What did British Prime Minister William Gladstone do to make some concession to the Irish?
   a. Increased taxes in Ireland
   b. Founded the Pan-Gaelic Cultural Festival
   c. Introduced the Irish Coercion Law
   d. Disestablished the Church of Ireland

5. The Irish National Land League was headed by whom?
   a. Daniel O'Connell
   b. Michael Collins
   c. Eamon de Valera
   d. Charles Stewart Parnell

6. What did the Irish Coercion Law do?
   a. Granted more rights to Irish tenants
   b. Gave police greater power to suppress Land League agitation
   c. Established the Land Commission
   d. Banned the use of the Irish language

7. Why were Charles Parnell and his associates arrested?
    a. For supporting the Coercion Law
    b. For participating in an armed rebellion
    c. For speaking out against the new law
    d. For advocating for British rule in Ireland

8. Which treaty brought the government and the Irish National Land League to an agreement?
    a. Kilmainham Treaty
    b. Treaty of Tallaght
    c. Anglo-Irish Treaty
    d. Treaty of Limerick

9. How did the Plan of Campaign help Irish farmers?
    a. It forced landlords to meet with their tenants to negotiate
    b. It decreased taxes on agricultural products
    c. It allowed landlords to evict tenants without cause
    d. It offered financial support to farmers

10. John Shinnick's death occurred during what event?
    a. Bunratty Massacre
    b. Land War
    c. Mitchelstown Massacre
    d. Tithe War

II. *True or False: Select whether each statement is correct or not.*

11. _____ Irish living abroad in other countries were completely cut off from their homeland and had no idea what was going on back in Ireland.

12. _____ Those who worked in this joint IRB-Fenian Brotherhood alliance were known as Fenians.

13. _____ The rebellion was discovered by the British when the employees of the *Irish People* accidentally lost the plans for the rebellion in a train station.

14. _____ The Fenian Uprising was foiled because the authorities had infiltrated the ranks of the Fenians with spies and informers.

15. _____ Fenians in Manchester were killed trying to rescue Thomas J. Kelly from a police van.

16. _____ "Agitation" meant causing civil disturbances without actually breaking the laws.

17. _____ The Land War was not an actual war, but a period of civil unrest and protest.

18. _____ The No Rent Manifesto called on all Irish landlords to stop charging their tenants rent.

19. _____ In a letter called *Saepe Nos*, Pope Leo condemned the Plan of Campaign.

20. _____ Farmers, politicians, and revolutionaries all joined forces to fight for fair rents using a variety of methods, including publishing newspapers, forming protective tenant leagues, mass protests, and even violence.

In a paragraph of six to none sentences, explain how the events in this unit contributed to the evolving dynamics of land conflicts, independence movements, and political unrest in Ireland during the 19th century.

Unit 8: Independence (Chap. 27-30)

Chapter 27: Home Rule   / 20 = _____%

I. Fill in the blank with the correct word from the word box.

World War I   Carson and Craig   Unionists   United Kingdom   Rome Rule   IPP
Liberal   Three   Home Rule   John Redmond   Nationalists

1. William Gladstone introduced the First _____ Bill in 1886.

2. Home Rule was opposed by those known as _____, because they favored keeping the current union with Great Britain.

3. The Unionists mockingly called Home Rule "_____," meaning that if Ireland became self-governing, the Catholic Church would gain power over Ireland's political interests.

4. British voters returned Gladstone's _____ party to power, and Gladstone immediately set about trying to pass Home Rule a second time.

5. The _____ was split into factions, some rallying behind Charles Stewart Parnell, and others opposing him.

6. After being introduced _____ times, Home Rule Bill was finally passed by the British Parliament.

7. The leader of the IPP at this time was _____.

8. _____ demanded that Ulster be permanently exempted from any Home Rule settlement.

9. _____ united the Unionist and Nationalist forces, as both of them considered the German Empire an existential threat to the United Kingdom.

10. While the majority of Irish supported the war in general, the _____ had more reservations, as they worried about how it would delay Home Rule.

11. World War I was a challenging time for Ireland, as it forced Irish Nationalists to balance their support for Home Rule against the necessity of defending the _____ from the German Empire.

II. Matching: Match the term with the correct definition.

1. _____ Home Rule

2. _____ Home Government Association

3. _____ The Local Government for Ireland Act

4. _____ The Parliament Act

5. _____ The Ulster Covenant

6. _____ Ulster and Irish Volunteers

7. _____ Ernest Edward Thomas

8. _____ Constructive unionism

9. _____ Grand juries

a. Organization founded by Isaac Butt

b. Removed House of Lords veto power

c. Two rival militias

d. Ireland self-governing within the U.K.

e. Made grand juries popularly elected

f. Fixing Irish problems through legislation

g. A body made of important landowners

h. Called Home Rule a conspiracy to
   eliminate religious freedom

i. The Anglo-Irish corporal who fired the
   first shot of WWI on the Western Front

I. Multiple Choice: Select the best answer from the choices provided.

1. What did "England's difficulty is Ireland's opportunity" mean?
    a. It referred to an economic partnership between England and Ireland
    b. It suggested that England's prosperity would benefit Ireland
    c. It indicated a desire for cooperation between England and Ireland
    d. Since England was fighting in WWI they would be less involved in Ireland

2. What job did the IRB's Military Council have?
    a. Oversee the training of the Volunteers
    b. Negotiate with British authorities
    c. Manage agricultural policies
    d. Launch an attack on British naval stations

3. How did the IRB Military Council intend to keep their plan from being leaked?
    a. Publicize their plan widely
    b. Share details with multiple individuals
    c. Tell as few people as possible
    d. Seek approval from the British government

4. Which day did the Easter Rising begin?
    a. Good Friday
    b. Holy Saturday
    c. Easter Sunday
    d. Easter Monday

5. Why was the turnout for the Easter Rising meager, outside of Dublin?
    a. Lack of interest among Irish citizens
    b. Ineffective communication of the rebellion's plans
    c. Eoin MacNeill sent a message to the Volunteers telling them not to fight
    d. Successful British propaganda

6. Who introduced the motion in Parliament that urged the Irish and British to compromise a solution to their conflicts?
    a. Éamon de Valera
    b. John Redmond
    c. Michael Collins
    d. Arthur Griffin

7. Which party took control of Parliament under Prime Minister Lloyd George?
    a. Conservative Party
    b. Labour Party
    c. Liberal Party
    d. Unionist Party

8. What was Sinn Féin founded as?
    a. A Marxist movement
    b. A nationalist political party
    c. A pro-British political party
    d. A paramilitary organization

9. Who was chosen President of the Republic?
    a. Éamon de Valera
    b. Michael Collins
    c. Arthur Griffin
    d. James Connolly

10. What was Britain's response to IRA violence?
    a. Establishing diplomatic relations with Ireland
    b. Creating the Black and Tans
    c. Implementing a policy of appeasement
    d. Forming the Auxiliary Division (Auxies)

II. True or False: Select whether each statement is correct or not.

11. _____ The IRB decided to stage a rising during the war and to seek the aid of Germany.

12. _____ The IRB tried to orchestrate a plot to smuggle Germans into England to overthrow the British Parliament.

13. _____ The Volunteers did not realize they were being trained for an actual rising, nor did the Military Council tell the IRB command this was their purpose.

14. _____ By Sunday after the Easter Rising, the British were back in control of Dublin.

15. _____ The British declared martial law while Lord Wimborne's troops began attacking Belfast.

16. _____ Ninety rebel leaders were sentenced to death.

17. _____ Britain realized how unpopular the executions of rebel leaders were but continued with them anyway.

18. _____ Lloyd George's government announced that Britain was implementing Home Rule in Ireland with no strings attached so Ireland could finally be completely independent.

19. _____ Martial law was declared in Munster and the British regular army was deployed in huge numbers.

20. _____ Eventually, Éamon de Valera met with representatives of the British government and military and the two sides finally agreed to a ceasefire.

I. Fill in the blank with the correct word from the word box.

Government of Ireland Act	Frank Aiken	Irish Civil War	Dominion
Four Courts	Liam Lynch	Sinn Féin	

1. The British wanted to grant Ireland _____ status, allowing Ireland to become a self-governing state within the British Empire.

2. During the war, the British Parliament had passed a bill known as the _____, splitting Ireland into two.

3. Anti-Treaty forces began protests and occupied the _____ of Dublin, Ireland's judicial center.

4. Michael Collins' Pro-Treaty _____ party won the election.

5. The shelling of the Four Courts began the _____.

6. _____ commanded the military of the Anti-Treaty forces against Collins.

7. Twenty days after Lynch's death, his successor _____ urged the remaining Anti-Treaty fighters to lay down their arms.

II. True or False: Select whether each statement is correct or not.

8. _____ All the negotiators agreed that accepting the Anglo-Irish Treaty was a good idea.

9. _____ The Anglo-Irish Treaty established the Irish Free State as a dominion of the British Empire.

10. _____ The Provisional Government of Ireland was supposed to oversee the transition of power from the British to the new Free State.

11. _____ When it came time for Collins to start building a military for the Free State he drew on Anti-Treaty Republicans to staff the army.

12. _____ The IRA voted that the Dáil did not have the authority to dissolve the republic.

13. _____ Most southern IRA units aligned with the Pro-Treaty forces, who were led by Michael Collins.

14. _____ Michael Collins was an Ulster Protestant who was opposed to Catholicism.

15. _____ In response to guerilla attacks from Lynch's forces, the Provisional Government began executing Anti-Treaty prisoners,.

I. Multiple Choice: Select the best answer from the choices provided.

1. What happened when Éamon de Valera emerged from hiding to campaign for the seat for County Clare?
    a. He won the presidency unopposed
    b. He was arrested
    c. He joined Cumann na nGaedheal
    d. He formed a coalition with the British government

2. Where was de Valera banned from going to?
    a. Dublin
    b. Connacht
    c. Ulster
    d. The United Kingdom

3. What treaty allowed Northern Ireland to opt out of the Free State?
    a. Anglo-Irish Treaty
    b. Treaty of Limerick
    c. Treaty of Versailles
    d. Anglo-French Treaty

4. Which of these was one of Cosgrave's first acts as President of the Executive Council?
    a. Increase the power of the County Councils
    b. Reduce the power of the County Councils
    c. Establish an independent judiciary
    d. Expand the role of the monarchy

5. What did Cumann na nGaedheal **not** do during Cosgrave's term?
    a. Restrain Catholic liberties
    b. Lower income taxes
    c. Invest in infrastructure projects
    d. Support agricultural exports

6. Who did the IRA make ties with as they drifted politically to the left?
    a. Monarchists
    b. Fascists
    c. Conservatives
    d. Socialists and communists

7. The IRA famously assassinated this Free State official in July, 1927:
    a. Michael Collins
    b. Kevin O'Higgins
    c. Éamon de Valera
    d. Arthur Griffin

8. What did Cosgrave's law mandate all candidates for the Dáil to do?
    a. Take the Oath of Allegiance
    b. Repudiate Sinn Féin
    c. Speak fluent Irish
    d. Denounce their political affiliations

9. Why did de Valera take the Oath of Allegiance?
    a. To get into government
    b. To enter Northern Ireland
    c. To gain support from the British Prime Minister
    d. To secure military aid

10. What was one of the reasons behind Cumann na nGaedheal losing support?
    a. Support for Anti-Treaty Republicans
    b. Opposition to the Anglo-Irish Treaty
    c. Cosgrave persecuted Anti-Treaty Republicans
    d. Cosgrave's support for socialism

11. Who struck the Oath of Supremacy from the Free State constitution?
    a. Arthur Griffin
    b. Michael Collins
    c. Richard Mulcahy
    d. Éamon de Valera

12. After independence, most Catholic clergy were
    a. Unionists
    b. Anti-Treaty
    c. Fianna Fáil
    d. Pro-Treaty

II. Matching: Match the term with the correct definition.

13. ____ Cumann na nGaedheal

14. ____ Hunger strike

15. ____ Fianna Fáil

16. ____ Governor General

17. ____ Oireachtas

18. ____ Oath of Allegiance

19. ____ Blueshirts

20. ____ 31st International Eucharistic Congress

a. U.K. representative in the Free State
b. De Valera founded this political party
c. Paramilitary group
d. Catholic assembly hosted by de Valera
e. The legislature of the Free State
f. Mandated by the Anglo-Irish Treaty
g. Governed the Free State during the 20s
h. To protest something by not eating

In an essay of six to nine sentences, explain how the Anglo-Irish Treaty became a source of division within the new Irish Free State.

Unit 9: Age of Trouble (Chap. 31-33)

Chapter 31: Northern Ireland   / 20 = _____%

I. Multiple Choice: Select the best answer from the choices provided.

1. What would Southern Ireland become after the Anglo-Irish Treaty?
    a. The Irish Republic
    b. The United Kingdom of Ireland
    c. The Irish Free State
    d. The Dominion of Erin

2. What did six Unionist counties of Ulster become?
    a. Northern Ireland
    b. The Republic of Ulster
    c. The Irish Free State
    d. The Connacht Province

3. Which act allowed the authorities to take any measure necessary to stop the IRA?
    a. Emergency Powers Act
    b. Counterterrorism Act
    c. Special Powers Act
    d. Defense of the Realm Act

4. Why were the specific six counties of Ulster chosen to be the nucleus of Northern Ireland?
    a. They had the highest Catholic population
    b. They were selected at random
    c. They were the only six counties that Unionists could hold
    d. They were strategically important for trade

5. The Commission held in London in 1924-1925 was meant to settle what?
    a. The legal status of Ulster Catholics
    b. The issue with the Oath of Allegiance
    c. The boundaries between the Free State and Northern Ireland
    d. The Free State's trade agreement with the U.K.

6. Who was the first Prime Minister of Northern Ireland?
    a. Michael Collins.
    b. Éamon de Valera
    c. Arthur Griffith
    d. James Craig

7. What group was banned in Northern Ireland?
    a. Ulster Volunteer Force
    b. Irish National Liberation Army
    c. Black and Tans
    d. Sinn Féin

8. Cosgrave yielded on the boundary question in exchange for Britian
    a. Renegotiating a trade deal with Ireland
    b. Forgiving Ireland's debt
    c. Providing the Free State with weapons
    d. Ratifying a military alliance

9. What does plural voting mean?
    a. People get multiple votes depending on their status
    b. Voting for multiple candidates in one election
    c. Voting by proxy
    d. Multiple people voting at one time

10. How were refugees of the Belfast Blitz treated by the Southern Irish?
    a. They were forcibly repatriated
    b. They were attended to and cared for
    c. They were met with hostility
    d. They were ignored and left to fend for themselves

I. Fill in the blank with the correct word from the word box.

| Gerrymandered | Donegal | Peace lines | W.T. Cosgrave | Unity | Belfast |
| Nationalists | Ulster Unionist Party | Boundary Commission | United Kingdom | | |

11. Most Irish Nationalists believed in the _____ of Ireland, that is, that Ireland the country and Ireland the island were one and the same.

12. Riots broke out in Derry after _____ took control of ten city councils in the elections.

13. When the Irish saw that giving up _____ to Northern Ireland was being discussed, they were outraged.

14. President _____ got the idea to try to negotiate the boundary using Ireland's debt to the United Kingdom.

15. In the end, the _____ made no substantial changes to the borders of the Free State and Northern Ireland.

16. In Northern Ireland, election wards were _____ to ensure permanent Unionist majorities.

17. In the Parliament of Northern Ireland, the government was dominated by the _____.

18. _____ were barriers made of brick, steel, or concrete, separating Protestant and Catholic neighborhoods.

19. Since Northern Ireland was part of the _____ but the rest of Ireland was not, this meant that Northern Ireland was at war with Germany during World War II, while the remainder of Ireland was at peace.

20. The Germans bombed _____ a total of four times, killing 900 people and injuring 1,500 more.

I. Multiple Choice: Select the best answer from the choices provided.

1. Why did the Parliament Great Britain pass the Statute of Westminster?
    a. To avoid legal conflict between the Parliament and the government of Ireland
    b. To strengthen its control over the dominions
    c. To limit the powers of the dominions
    d. To merge the dominions into a single entity

2. From whom did Éamon de Valera seek input about his new constitution?
    a. International legal scholars
    b. Religious leaders
    c. British government officials
    d. Military leaders

3. What did the Vatican Secretary of State, Cardinal Eugenio Pacelli, say about de Valera's constitution?
    a. "We shall maintain silence."
    b. "Strongly endorse and support."
    c. "Strongly disapprove."
    d. "Advocate for immediate changes."

4. What did the constitution change the country's name, Irish Free State, to?
    a. Hibernia
    b. Gaelic Republic
    c. Éire
    d. Republic of Ireland

5. Why didn't de Valera want to enter World War II on the Allied side?
    a. He was wary of getting the Republic into a war since it was so new
    b. He believed in the ideals of the Axis powers
    c. He sought to remain neutral in all conflicts
    d. He wanted to support the Allied powers but faced internal opposition

6. What did the IRA do to cause arrests of the active members?
    a. Engaged in humanitarian efforts
    b. Advocated for peace
    c. Collaborated with the Allies
    d. Tried to ally with the Nazis

7. What was the result of Éamon de Valera formally declaring Ireland a republic?
    a. Joining the British Commonwealth
    b. Establishing a monarchy
    c. Leaving the British Commonwealth
    d. Joining the League of Nations

8. Who greatly helped Ireland's economy expand?
    a. Winston Churchill
    b. Seán Lemass
    c. Éamon de Valera
    d. Michael Collins

9. What did de Valera hope for Ireland?
    a. Continued partition
    b. Annexation by the United Kingdom
    c. Established of a monarchy
    d. Reunification of North and South

10. Where was Éamon de Valera buried?
    a. Béal na Bláth
    b. Soloheadbeg
    c. Glasnevin
    d. Knockmealdown

II. Matching: Match the term with the correct definition.

11. _____ Statute of Westminster

12. _____ Taoiseach

13. _____ President of Ireland

14. _____ Republic of Ireland Act

15. _____ Fine Gael

a. Head of State
b. Led Ireland through most of the 50s
c. Head of Government
d. Officially removed Ireland from the British Commonwealth
e. Removed authority of Great Britain over its six dominions

I. True or False: Select whether each statement is correct or not.

1. _____ After World War II, the leaders of the IRA resolved to completely separate from Sinn Féin.

2. _____ During the Border Campaign, some IRA members accidentally blew themselves up while constructing bombs.

3. _____ Fine Gael and de Valera were forgiving to the IRA members, seeing no reason to punish them.

4. _____ Sinn Féin's leadership began embracing Marxism and leftist causes.

5. _____ Tony Magan resigned from the IRA over disagreements about the group's relations with Sinn Féin.

6. _____ The beatings of Catholics in Derry were filmed by journalists and broadcast all over the world, resulting in outrage among Catholics and nationalists.

7. _____ The Lynch government set up field hospitals along the border to aid the wounded and requested U.N. Peacekeepers to quell the violence.

8. _____ Military units from Scotland were deployed to Belfast to restore order.

9. _____ The Royal Ulster Constabulary maintained neutrality throughout the Troubles.

10. _____ The British military imposed curfews over entire neighborhoods and the introduction of mass arrests without trial.

II. Fill in the blank with the correct word from the word box.

| Free Derry | Bloody Sunday | Ian Paisley | Jack Lynch | Prohibited | Border Campaign |
| Battle of the Bogside | | Tony Magan | Peace Lines | African Americans | |

11. After the union of Sinn Féin and the IRA, _____ pushed for the IRA to re-arm.

12. The aim of the _____ was to use guerilla tactics to attack British military until it became impossible for the British to govern Northern Ireland.

13. _____ hoped to strengthen bonds with Northern Ireland so that the two governments could collaborate on issues such as trade, agriculture, and tourism.

14. _____ convinced U.K. loyalists that the Easter Rising parades were a front for a new campaign by the IRA.

15. Inspired by the civil rights movement of _____ in the United States, Catholics in Northern Ireland launched their own civil rights movement.

16. Catholics of Bogside barricaded all entries to their neighborhoods, creating "_____," a zone where the Ulster police were physically prevented from entering.

17. The fight between the Apprentice Boys and the Catholics at Bogside lasted three full days and is known as the _____.

18. The Northern Irish government and British military decided on the construction of _____ to prevent violence against Catholics.

19. _____ began as a civil rights march in Derry organized by the Northern Ireland Civil Rights Association.

20. Protestors showed up to the Derry civil rights march despite it being _____ and began pelting British soldiers with stones.

In a paragraph of six to nine sentences, describe the key historical events leading to the outbreak of the Troubles.

Unit 10: Ireland Today (Chap. 34-35)

Chapter 34: Direct Rule / 15 _____ %

I. Multiple Choice: Select the best answer from the choices provided.

1. What did the Northern Ireland Temporary Provisions Act do?
   a. Suspended the Parliament of Northern Ireland
   b. Expanded the powers of the Parliament of Northern Ireland
   c. Established an independent Northern Ireland government
   d. Dissolved the Parliament of Northern Ireland

2. Which 1973 agreement created a new legislative assembly for Northern Ireland?
   a. The Sunningdale Agreement
   b. The Downing Street Declaration
   c. The Belfast Agreement
   d. The Good Friday Agreement

3. What would be the purpose of the Council of Ireland that British Prime Minister Heath wanted to create?
   a. Oversee only issues in Northern Ireland
   b. Act as an advisory body with no decision-making power
   c. Work on issues that affected the entire island
   d. Reunify Northern Ireland with the Republic

4. Who formed the organization Community of Peace People and won a Nobel Peace Prize?
   a. Gerry Adams
   b. Betty Williams
   c. David Trimble
   d. John Hume

5. Why did Britain establish Diplock courts in Northern Ireland?
   a. To speed up the legal process
   b. Because juries were being threatened
   c. To increase transparency in the legal system
   d. To address the concerns of jury bias

6. How did the government prevent protests against any proposed Anglo-Irish Agreement?
    a. By allowing protests without any restrictions
    b. By implementing curfews
    c. By deploying the military to suppress protests
    d. By not implementing any agreement unless the majority voted for it

7. What does the Anglo-Irish Agreement of 1985 say?
    a. The North would cut off diplomatic ties with the Republic
    b. British administrators would have no role in Northern Ireland
    c. Northern Ireland could unilaterally secede from the U.K.
    d. British administrators of Northern Ireland would meet regularly with the Republic to cooperate on certain issues

8. He was the first to die during the 1981 Hunger Strikes.
    a. Brian Faulkner
    b. Alan Black
    c. Bobby Sands
    d. Garret FitzGerald

II. True or False: Select whether each statement is correct or not.

9. _____ When the Republic refused to amend Articles 2 and 3 from its constitution, Unionists formally withdrew their support from the Sunningdale Agreement.

10. _____ The men who were gunned down in the Kingsmill Massacre were Protestants.

11. _____ Nobody died during the hunger strike of 1981.

12. _____ The British authorities agreed to most of the hunger strikers' demands.

13. _____ Prime Minister Margaret Thatcher decided that severing Northern Ireland from the U.K. was the best course of action.

14. _____ The ratification of the 1985 Anglo-Irish Agreement led to the violence of the Troubles getting much worse.

15. _____ The Taoiseach who signed the 1985 Anglo-Irish Agreement was Garret FitzGerald.

I. True or False: Select whether each statement is correct or not.

1. _____ Following the IRA ceasefire, the Ulster Volunteer Force, Ulster Defence Association, and other unionist paramilitary forces announced their own ceasefires as well.

2. _____ One hour after the IRA announced an end to their ceasefire, they detonated a bomb in a rail station in London.

3. _____ A survey by the newspaper *Belfast Telegraph* revealed that optimism for a peace settlement was extremely high, with most Catholics and Protestants believing a solution was at hand.

4. _____ Surveys in Ireland showed that large majorities on both sides of the border opposed the Good Friday Agreement.

5. _____ The rest of the world supported the Good Friday Agreement.

II. Fill in the blank with the correct word from the word box.

Sinn Féin   Good Friday Agreement   Ceasefire   Anglo-Irish Agreement   The Troubles
Tony Blair   Ian Paisley   Republicans   Omagh   Joint Declaration of Peace

6. The British authorities, Gerry Adams, and John Hume discussed ways to peaceably end _____.

7. The electoral successes of Sinn Féin convinced _____ that their goals might be better achieved through the political process than through violence.

8. _____founded a political party called the Democratic Unionist Party.

9. Paisley believed that the _____ was a prelude to the reunification of Ireland and persecution of Protestants by the island's Catholic majority.

10. The Provisional IRA announced a _____ when they realized they could not beat the British military.

11. British Prime Minister John Major and Taoiseach Albert Reynolds issued the _____.

12. The new Labour Prime Minister _____ was an ardent supporter of the peace process.

13. Part of the _____ was that the religious liberty of all must be respected.

14. The _____ bombing provoked international outrage and only strengthened resolve for the peace process to continue.

15. John Major said he would refuse to allow _____ to participate in peace talks until the IRA completely disarmed.

In a paragraph of six to nine sentences, discuss how economic growth, paramilitary disarmament, and European Union involvement all contributed to strengthening Ireland following the Good Friday Agreement.

Chapter 1: The Shores of Hibernia

1. A
2. C
3. D
4. A
5. B
6. C
7. B
8. A
9. C
10. D

11. F
12. F
13. F
14. T
15. T

Chapter 2: Gaelic Society

1. F
2. F
3. T
4. T
5. F
6. F
7. T
8. T
9. T
10. T

11. B
12. F
13. J
14. I
15. G
16. A
17. E
18. C
19. D
20. H

Chapter 3: The Otherworld

1. A
2. C
3. B
4. D
5. B
6. C
7. A
8. B
9. D
10. A

11. Dagda
12. Ériu
13. Cernunnos
14. Dead
15. Sea
16. Druids
17. Samhain
18. Imbolc
19. Bealtaine
20. Lughnasadh

Chapter 4: Arrival of Christianity

1. T
2. F
3. F
4. T
5. T
6. T
7. T

8. A
9. C
10. D
11. B
12. B
13. A
14. D
15. D

Chapter 5: The Mission of St. Patrick

1. D
2. B
3. C
4. A
5. A
6. B
7. D
8. C
9. A
10. B

11. T
12. F
13. T
14. F
15. T
16. T
17. T
18. T
19. T
20. F

Chapter 6: The Great Founders

1. B
2. B
3. A
4. C
5. D
6. D
7. C
8. B
9. A
10. C
11. C

12. Monasticism
13. Inishmore
14. Limestone
15. Clonard
16. Penitential
17. Half-free
18. Church of Oak
19. Scotland
20. Conleth

Chapter 7: The Twilight of Paganism

1. T
2. F
3. F
4. T
5. T
6. F

7. D
8. B
9. B
10. C
11. A
12. C
13. B
14. B
15. A

Chapter 8: Diarmait mac Cerbaill

1. A
2. D
3. C
4. A
5. A
6. B
7. D
8. C
9. A
10. D
11. C
12. D
13. A

14. E
15. B
16. G
17. C
18. F
19. A
20. D

Chapter 9: The Missionaries

1. St. Columba
2. Ireland
3. Iona
4. Áedán

5. Illumination
6. Scotland
7. Dál Riata
8. Church
9. St. Columbanus
10. Agilulf

11. T
12. T
13. F
14. T
15. T
16. F
17. T
18. T
19. F
20. T

Chapter 10: Literature & Church

1. A
2. C
3. D
4. B
5. C
6. A
7. A
8. D
9. B
10. B
11. D
12. C
13. A

14. T
15. T
16. T
17. F
18. T
19. T
20. F

Chapter 11: The Irish in England

1. British Isles
2. Roman Empire
3. Britain
4. Anglo-Saxons
5. Augustine
6. Canterbury
7. Northumbria
8. Oswald
9. Columba
10. Benedictine

11. T
12. F
13. T
14. T
15. F
16. T
17. T
18. T
19. F
20. F

Chapter 12: The Age of the Vikings

1. T
2. T
3. F
4. T
5. F
6. F
7. T
8. T
9. F
10. T

11. B
12. D
13. A
14. C
15. B
16. B
17. A

18. D
19. C
20. D

Chapter 13: Brian Ború

1. C
2. A
3. C
4. D
5. B
6. C
7. D
8. A
9. C
10. B

11. Province
12. Dal Cais
13. Sulcoit
14. Máel Muad
15. Eoganachta
16. High King
17. Church
18. Apostolic City
19. Norse
20. Uí Dúnlainge

Chapter 14: Struggling for Unity

1. F
2. T
3. F
4. T
5. T
6. T
7. F
8. F
9. F
10. T
11. F
12. T

13. E
14. H
15. A
16. D
17. G
18. B
19. F
20. C

Chapter 15: Strongbow & Henry

1. Richard de Clare
2. Waterford
3. High King Rory
4. Diarmait
5. Leinster
6. Henry
7. Royal Constable
8. Northern Uí Néill
9. Pope Alexander III

10. A
11. C
12. B
13. D
14. D
15. A

Chapter 16: The Norman Age

1. D
2. A
3. C
4. B
5. D
6. B
7. C
8. A
9. D
10. B
11. B

12. G
13. A

14. E
15. C
16. I
17. H
18. D
19. B
20. F

Chapter 17: Gaelic Resurgence

1. T
2. T
3. F
4. T
5. T
6. F
7. T
8. F
9. T
10. F
11. F
12. F
13. T
14. T

15. D
16. F
17. B
18. A
19. C
20. E

Chapter 18: The Wars of the Tudors

1. Wars of the Roses
2. Clanricarde
3. Poynings
4. Young Gerald
5. Act of Supremacy
6. Silken Thomas
7. Henry VIII
8. England
9. Church of Ireland
10. Ireland

11. D
12. B
13. B
14. B
15. A
16. D
17. C
18. C
19. A
20. A

Chapter 19: The Desmond Rebellion

1. C
2. A
3. C
4. D
5. B
6. D
7. C
8. A
9. B
10. D

11. F
12. T
13. T
14. F
15. F
16. T
17. T
18. T
19. F
20. F

Chapter 20: Dealing with Ulster

1. A
2. D
3. C
4. C
5. B
6. A
7. D
8. D

9. B
10. D

11. F
12. T
13. T
14. T
15. F

Chapter 21: The Wars of Cromwell

1. Irish Catholics
2. Strafford
3. Protestant
4. Conspirators
5. Bann
6. Parliamentarians
7. Confederates
8. Ormonde
9. Royalist
10. Drogheda
11. Cromwell
12. Kilkenny

13. B
14. H
15. F
16. C
17. E
18. A
19. D
20. G

Chapter 22: The Penal Laws

1. Charles II
2. Charles Coote
3. Test Act
4. Oliver Plunkett
5. King of England
6. Jacobite
7. Williamites
8. Enniskilliners
9. Penal

10. William III
11. T
12. T
13. F
14. F
15. T
16. F
17. T
18. F
19. T
20. T

Chapter 23: The Anglo-Irish

1. C
2. A
3. C
4. C
5. D
6. A
7. B
8. C
9. D
10. B
11. A
12. D
13. C
14. A

15. D
16. C
17. E
18. B
19. A
20. F

Chapter 24: The '98 & Daniel O'Connell

1. B
2. A
3. A
4. C
5. D
6. B

7. C

8. C

9. B

10. D

11. H

12. J

13. G

14. B

15. D

16. C

17. I

18. E

19. A

20. F

8. A

9. A

10. C

11. F

12. T

13. T

14. T

15. T

16. T

17. T

18. F

19. T

20. T

Chapter 25: The Potato Famine

1. England

2. Disenfranchised

3. Tithe War

4. Ireland

5. Spaniards/Spanish

6. Taxes

7. Whig

8. Poor Law

9. T

10. F

11. T

12. F

13. T

14. F

15. T

Chapter 26: Land Conflicts

1. C

2. A

3. D

4. D

5. D

6. B

7. C

Chapter 27: Home Rule

1. Home Rule

2. Unionists

3. Rome Rule

4. Liberal

5. IPP

6. Three

7. John Redmond

8. Carson and Craig

9. World War I

10. Nationalists

11. United Kingdom

12. D

13. A

14. E

15. B

16. H

17. C

18. I

19. F

20. G

Chapter 28: Easter Rising & War of Independence

1. D
2. A
3. C
4. D
5. C
6. B
7. C
8. B
9. A
10. B

11. T
12. F
13. T
14. T
15. F
16. T
17. F
18. F
19. T
20. T

Chapter 29: The Irish Civil War

1. Dominion
2. Government of Ireland Act
3. Four Courts
4. Sinn Féin
5. Irish Civil War
6. Liam Lynch
7. Frank Aiken

8. F
9. T
10. T
11. F
12. T
13. F
14. F
15. T

Chapter 30: The Irish Free State

1. B
2. C
3. A
4. B
5. A
6. D
7. B
8. A
9. A
10. C
11. D
12. D

13. G
14. H
15. B
16. A
17. E
18. F
19. C
20. D

Chapter 31: Northern Ireland

1. C
2. A
3. C
4. C
5. C
6. D
7. D
8. B
9. A
10. B

11. Unity
12. Nationalists
13. Donegal
14. W.T. Cosgrave
15. Boundary Commission
16. Gerrymandered
17. Ulster Unionist Party

18. Peace Lines
19. United Kingdom
20. Belfast

Chapter 32: The Republic of Ireland

1. A
2. B
3. A
4. C
5. A
6. D
7. C
8. B
9. D
10. C

11. E
12. C
13. A
14. D
15. B

Chapter 33: The Troubles

1. F
2. T
3. F
4. T
5. T
6. T
7. T
8. F
9. F
10. T

11. Tony Magan
12. Border Campaign
13. Jack Lynch
14. Ian Paisely
15. African Americans
16 Free Derry

17. Battle of the Bogside
18. Peace Lines
19. Bloody Sunday
20. Prohibited

Chapter 34: Direct Rule

1. A
2. A
3. C
4. B
5. B
6. D
7. D
8. C

9. T
10. T
11. F
12. T
13. F
14. F
15. T

Chapter 35: The Good Friday Agreement

1. T
2. T
3. F
4. F
5. T

6. The Troubles
7. Violence
8. Ian Paisley
9. Anglo-Irish Agreement
10. Ceasefire
11. Joint Declaration of Peace
12. Tony Blair
13. Good Friday Agreement
14. Omagh
15. Sinn Féin

Unit 1 Essay Question Answer Key

Sample answer:

Status was important to the ancient Gaels; in fact, their entire society was structured around status and social distinctions. For example, every ruler was part of a hierarchy that determined his level of influence: there were petty kings (rí tuaithe) who had to answer to a higher king (ruirí), who in turn had to answer to a provincial king (rí coiced). Communities too had status, from clans to coiceda and up to the kingdoms (tuatha). Individuals, too, all had a status which determined their legal rights. At the bottom were slaves, who were property. Then there were the "half-free," the freedmen, and finally free persons, who were not in bondage to anybody. Warriors, too, were a special caste, either subject to a king or free (fianna). At the top of the caste were the Druids, who had a special status as mediators with the gods. They were the lorekeepers of the Gaels and were even above kings in their influence. All in all, Gaelic society was dominated by the idea of status, in which everybody had a specifically designated place in the social hierarchy.

Unit 2 Essay Question Answer Key

Sample answer:

The transition from Druidic paganism to Christianity in Ireland was a gradual process influenced by several factors. First, the example of influential hermits, like, St. Kevin, who, though born into pagan nobility, embraced Christianity, lived a life of asceticism, and established a monastery. Then there were royal conversions, such as that of Óengus mac Nad Froích and Diarmait mac Cerbaill. These kings played a crucial role in encouraging the adoption of Christianity by the ruling class. The Convention of Drumceat showed the balance between preserving Gaelic traditions and accommodating Christianity, allowing the bardic tradition to persist. This transition was not marked by hostility, demonstrating a coexistence between Druidic and Christian influences in Ireland.

Unit 3 Essay Question Answer Key

Sample answer:

Ireland played a crucial role in spreading Christianity to other kingdoms and regions through the efforts of missionaries like St. Columba, St. Columbanus, and St. Aidan. After its conversion to Christianity, Ireland would produce many missionaries who would travel to other lands. St. Columba's monastery on Iona became a center for spreading Christianity to the Picts in Scotland, showcasing the Irish missionaries' commitment to reaching neighboring regions. St. Columbanus went to France and later to Italy, founding monasteries and converting local tribes. In England, St. Aidan's work in Northumbria left a permanent mark on the Christianization of the Anglo-Saxon kingdoms. What set these Irish missionaries apart was their ability to adapt to local customs, making Christianity more accessible and relevant to diverse populations. Their efforts not only led to widespread conversions but also influenced the cultural and religious landscape of the regions they explored, solidifying Ireland's significant role in the growth of Christianity.

Unit 4 Essay Question Answer Key

During the high Middle Ages, the Irish ultimately failed to unify their island into a single kingdom despite the fact that many other European kingdoms were doing just that. Two major reasons for this are foreign invasions and squabbling among the Irish kings themselves. From the 8th to the 11th century, Ireland was invaded by successive waves of Vikings. The Vikings not only seized portions of Ireland for themselves, but also got involved in the squabbles of the Irish clans. Then in the 12th century the Normans came, getting involved in the way between High King Rory and Diarmait mac Murchada, eventually establishing control over Leinster. But perhaps a more important reason Ireland couldn't unite was because of the infighting amongst the Irish themselves. Even during the age of the Viking invasions, Irish-on-Irish violence outpaced Viking violence. Not even the great Brian Ború was able to completely put an end to the squabbling of the clans, and during the 12th century it was the rivalry between Rory and Diarmait mac Murchada that resulted in the Norman conquest. The Gaels were too prone to fighting one another.

Unit 5 Essay Question Answer Key

Sample answer:

The Wars of the Roses were a brutal civil conflict for control of the English throne between the houses of Lancaster and York, which led to the rise of the Tudors after Henry Tudor's victory at the Battle of Bosworth Field in 1485. Henry's victory marked the beginning of Tudor rule, which would have significant consequences for Ireland. The Tudors sought to strengthen English control in Ireland and undo the Gaelic gains of the previous century. They faced challenges from powerful Irish families like the Fitzgeralds, but after putting down the Kildare Rebellion, Henry was able to consolidate English authority. He did this through the establishment of the Church of Ireland aimed to solidify English authority. He also implemented the policy of surrender and regrant, where Irish lords surrendered their lands and received them back as vassals of Henry VIII. By the end of Henry VIII"s reign, English power had been substantially strengthened in Ireland.

Unit 6 Essay Question Answer Key

Sample answer:

The Cromwellian conquest of Ireland, marked by harsh measures and land confiscations, followed by the imposition of the Penal Laws, significantly altered the fabric of 17th-century Irish society. These events led to a drastic reduction in Catholic land ownership, forced emigration, and the suppression of religious freedom. The lasting consequences included political disenfranchisement of Catholics and Catholics having to turn to underground practices to preserve their faith. The practice of Catholicism was suspended in many parts of Ireland for months or years. It also resulted in the transfer of Catholics to the new world as indentured servants as a form of punishment for opposing the regime. The interaction of historical events such as the Restoration of the Stuarts, the Jacobite movement, and the Treaty of Limerick further increased the impact on Ireland and shaped its path for years to come.

Unit 7: Essay Question Answer Key

Sample answer:

The aftermath of the famine caused bitter land conflicts, changing the relationships between tenants and landlords. The emergence of organizations like the Fenian Brotherhood and the Irish Republican Brotherhood reflected the persistence of Irish independence movements. They also served to connected immigrant communities in the United States with events in their homeland. The Fenians' attempt at uprising, although a failure, sparked political ramifications and influenced British policy, notably leading to the Church of Ireland's disestablishment. Simultaneously, the worsening land problem fueled the rise of the Land League. The Land War, marked by civil unrest, culminated in the Plan of Campaign, a coordinated effort by Irish tenants against landlords. Despite the Kilmainham Treaty easing tensions temporarily, the underlying issues stayed.

Unit 8: Essay Question Answer Key

Sample answer:

The Anglo-Irish Treaty signed in 1921 established the Irish Free State as a dominion within the British Empire. The treaty would prove tremendously controversial, leading to the Irish Civil War. In the first place, the Treaty allowed six counties of Ulster to "opt out" of the Free State, remaining part of the United Kingdom. This was unpopular with Irish nationalists, who believed the island of Ireland was indivisible politically. Another source of contention was the Oath of Allegiance. Since the treaty kept the Free State within the British Empire, elected officials were compelled to swear an oath of allegiance to the British monarch. This fractured Irish politics. Sinn Féin considered the oath illegitimate and abstained from any participation in government, while de Valera founded Fianna Fáil to work within the framework of the Free State to eventually get the oath removed. Hostility between pro and anti-treaty forces was so intense that it led to the Irish Civil War, as anti-treaty forces believed Michael Collins' government was a puppet of the British. In the aftermath of the war, the Cosgrave government would continue to persecute republicans who had opposed the treaty.

Unit 9: Essay Question Answer Key

Sample answer:

There were several events that contributed to the outbreak of the Troubles. In the first place, the takeover of Sinn Féin by the IRA after World War II led to the rearming of the IRA and the Border Campaign, which unleashed a wave of violence in the border counties. Meanwhile

Catholics in Northern Ireland organized the Catholic Civil Rights Movement to protest discrimination. Northern Irish authorities responded to civil rights' events harshly, banning them or openly attacking them, as in the 1972 Bloody Sunday shootings. There was also agitation by U.K. royalists like Ian Paisely who were against any compromise with Catholics. Paisely formed the Ulster Constitution Defence Committee (UCDC) and the Ulster Protestant Volunteers (UPV), the latter of which engaged in acts of violence against Catholics. The hostility degenerated into riots, bombings, and assassinations, ushering in the age of the Troubles.

Unit 10: Essay Question Answer Key

Sample answer:

After the Good Friday Agreement, Ireland went through many important changes. The disarmament of the paramilitary groups between 2000 and 2010 allowed life to return to normal which was good for the region. Economically, the Republic of Ireland experienced a remarkable turnaround, evolving from one of Europe's poorest nations to one of its wealthiest during the period of the "Irish miracle." This was brought about largely by foreign investment from the United States. Low tax rates also encouraged the growth of business. Access to European Union funding also helped build Ireland's economy, as did adoption of the Euro currency. The growing economy helped stabilize the situation in Ireland, as people are much less likely to turn to violence when things are going well economically. Though Ireland is not without problems today—restrictive EU obligations, Brexit, and migration are all areas of concern—both the Republic and Northern Ireland are in a much better condition today than they were before the Good Friday Agreement.

www.ingramcontent.com/pod-product-compliance
Lightning Source LLC
Chambersburg PA
CBHW081234090426
42738CB00016B/3301